Recruiting Love

Using The Business Skills You Have to Find the Love You Want

by Alison Blackman Dunham &
Jessica Blackman Freedman
"The Advice Sisters"

Recruiting Love: Using the Business Skills You Have to Find the Love You Want

Copyright ©1998 by Alison Blackman Dunham and Jessica Blackman Freedman

All rights reserved. No part of this book may be reproduced or transmitted in any form for sale without written permission from the publisher, except for brief quotations included in a review.

This book is not intended as a substitute for professional therapy, and neither the authors nor the publisher assume any liability for damages incurred by following the advice contained or implied in this book.

Published by:
Cyclone Books
420 Pablo Lane
Nipomo, CA 93444
email: cyclone@lightspeed.net
Orders (888)678-3666

ISBN 1-890723-19-3
Library of Congress Catalog Number 98-071682

Library of Congress Cataloging-In-Publication Data
Dunham, Alison Blackman
Freedman, Jessica Blackman
Recruiting Love: Using The Business Skills You Have to Find the Love You Want
1. Relationships   2. Self-Help

To our husbands, Bruce and John and to our parents, Norman and Sylvia Blackman who taught us the meaning of true love.

...and to all singles seeking to reclaim their dignity.

Illustrations by Steve Spatucci and Daniel Crawford

Cover design by Tony Hubert of Trubeat
tony@trubeat.com

Author photos by Dawn Otten

4   Recruiting Love

The Advice Sisters exchanging pearls of wisdom

Introduction

The idea of using a business-type plan to find love has been developed out of more than 20 years of personal experience, and from the real stories of our friends, colleagues, and clients. Using our plan, adults can take control of their love search in the same way they have taken control of their careers and put an end to the helpless victim cycle.

We wrote this book primarily for single adults who want to be part of a heterosexual couple in an intimate, committed relationship (in many cases, leading to marriage). However, everything in the book also applies to same sex couples and people who wish to be in a loving, committed relationship without marriage. With this in mind, we have tried to use non-gender-sensitive language and examples wherever possible.

Recruiting Love was originally planned to be a funny book. Some of the personal accounts we've included are indeed humorous, but we found that looking for love just isn't a funny subject. For many adult singles it is a serious and sometimes painful experience. So instead, we wrote an *uplifting* book — one which will bring **real hope** with a plan that **really works**! There are no "quick-fixes" in *Recruiting Love* — to make the plan work you've got to *do* work — but **anyone** can follow this plan and succeed!

Contents

Introduction
What Makes *Recruiting Love* Different? 8
What Do I Have to Do to Make It Work? 8
I'm Looking for Love, Not an Employee! 10

Chapter 1: Outline for Action
Why Traditional Dating Methods Don't Work 17

Chapter 2: Creating the "You Company" Job Description
Creating The Job Description 29
Consider "Job Histories" 37

Chapter 3: Creating the "You Company" Profile 47

Chapter 4 Targeting the "You Company" Candidate Search
Networking for Love 70
The "Envisioning Exercise" 75
How to Target the Best Locales 78
How to Keep a Dating Log (& Why You Need To!) 85

Chapter 5: Covering All the Bases
The Singles Bar Scene 98
Singles Clubs and Groups 98
The Internet: Looking for Love In Cyberspace 105
Love in the Workplace 105
The "Personals" 106
Matchmakers and Dating Services 117

Introduction   7

Chapter 6: Tools to Facilitate the Search
The Answering Machine: a Recruiter's Best Friend 126
Manners Aren't Just for Amy Vanderbilt 131
Tools That Can (Literally) Save Your Life 132
The Dating Kit 133
Planning your Mental and Verbal Icebreakers 134
Fashion Tools 139

Chapter 7: Improving Your Interviewing Skills
How Much Do You Tell? 151
Safety Begins at Home 153
Interview Candidates at Your "Office" 154
Who Pays? 156
Make Your Friends Part of Your Date! (We Mean It!) 158
The Date is Over—Now What? 158
Savvy, Safe, Sex 161
Handling Dating Disasters 162

Chapter 8: Adjusting Your Recruitment Strategy
Analyze and Adjust Your Plan 181
Do These Stories Sound Familiar? 182
Tell "Mr. or Ms. Toad" to "Hit The Road" 200
Using Your Dating Log to Get Back on Track 200
Do You Need to Take a Break? 202
Find Support In a Dating Success Team 203
Starting Your Own Dating Success Team 204

Chapter 9: Making an Offer
How Do I Know If I Want to Make an Offer? 215
My Candidate is Reluctant to Accept My Job Offer 222
Should I Agree to Live Together? 223
My Candidate Turned the "Job" Down 225
How Can I Make My New Search Successful? 232
Some Final Thoughts on Your Journey: 237

What Makes Recruiting Love Different?

This book will not teach you how to flirt. It will not encourage you to play "hard to get," or any other games that should be left behind after high school. Unlike other dating guides, we didn't fill the book with endless psychological tests or pop-psychology lectures on why you should pick one person over another. Instead, through a unique business analogy, we show you how to stay focused, organized, and most of all, ACTIVE. We will change your way of thinking about your love search, and help you accomplish this challenging task with dignity, efficiency, and pleasure.

As you complete the "Action Memo" at the end of each chapter, you will be creating a personalized plan for finding love. As a love recruiter, **you** call the shots and **you** control your search. You will actively seek out and find love, not wait passively for love to find you. You will map out the most efficient route, planning step-by-step to "recruit" and "select" the love you really want.

What Do I Have to Do to Make It Work?

Like anything worth having, recruiting love takes hard work. We strongly believe it has to be your #1 priority (after staying alive and being responsible to your family and job) for as long as the search takes you. The plan won't work if you just read the first chapter, complete a couple of action memos, and then stay home and wait for something to happen. *Recruiting Love* works like any business plan — there are chronological steps you must research, plan, and follow. You set target dates, and stick to them as best as possible. You should **plan** and **schedule** your recruiting activities **every week**. Write them on your calendar (just like a business meeting) and (just like a business project) commit yourself to doing them. You can't just "try" at this — you have to DO it! The harder you work, the easier it gets, and the quicker you'll see results.

How Does Recruiting Love Work?

This book helps you select the kind of partner you want, determine where the best candidates are, and efficiently target your search using the **business skills** that you already have. Suppose you wanted to find whole wheat bread at the supermarket. It wouldn't be very efficient to walk up and down every aisle wishing and hoping to find the perfect loaf. You would find the bread aisle, select a few brands from the endless varieties on display, and (after considering price, size, etc.) select the loaf that's right for you. That's also the idea of our book — we don't tell you what kind of person would be best for you, but we do show you how you can maximize your chances of finding that person, without walking up and down infinite aisles of toads!

But Won't This Take Time and Effort?

If you've stuck with us this far, you're probably a successful professional (or well on your way!) and have undoubtedly put in some long hours at the office. Why wouldn't you work just as hard to reach your personal goals? Each love search is unique, so we can't tell you exactly how long it will take. We can say that the time and effort you put into recruiting love is a lifetime investment. If it takes you a while, it's not much when you consider that reaching **this** goal will continue to reap rewards for as long as you live! (Can you really say that about all your overtime at the office?)

If you've looked for a job before, you'll find that recruiting love requires activities similar to those you've already used in business. The difference is that in *this* search, you're the recruiter and the employer, and your potential dates are your job "candidates!"

Why The Business Analogy?
I'm Looking for Love, Not an Employee!

With *Recruiting Love*, you make the decisions, and you choose the candidate. As a love recruiter, you can **make** love happen through identifying what you want, knowing what you have to offer, planning and targeting your search, and using the appropriate tools (which we provide throughout the book). It's a challenging process, but not an overwhelming or humiliating one, because you have active control over the entire campaign!

This Sounds so Calculating!
I Thought Love was About Feelings!

Don't misunderstand us. We're not saying the love search is **exactly** like the business deal. We know that no matter how carefully you plan, there still needs to be that "spark" that (hopefully!) you won't find in any job search! But a spark should be just that — a spark — and not a blinding light! The divorce rate is staggering 50 percent. Many of these divorces break up families and severely impact children. It may not seem very romantic, but the statistics prove that we DO need to put more thought into the love search.

There are plenty of more romantic dating guides out there, but what good is a ring or a "yes" if you're headed for divorce court later?

But How Do I Know What I Really Want?

The *Recruiting Love* plan assumes that as an adult, you can decide what you want. To help you clarify your vision and make it complete, we will give you some thought-provoking exercises, but we won't talk down to you or use pop-psychology to create easy answers. If you are looking for that, there are already plenty of books. (However, those books won't help you target, locate, and recruit someone special.)

Take inspiration from the "Bottom Line" aphorisms, and true stories throughout the book. These stories are from people just like you — people who have invested too much time in their high school dating techniques, and who have kissed their share (or more) of toads!

For professional recruiters, there is no more satisfying reward than finding the perfect match for a position. For you, as a love-recruiter, there's nothing more satisfying than being with the partner you've planned for, dreamed about, and worked so hard to find. Good luck and happy hunting!

THE BOTTOM LINE
"Each journey begins with one small step." Anonymous

And this is my fourth favorite cheer from high school!

From the desk of: The Advice Sisters

TO: *You Company* Recruiter

FROM: Alison and Jessica

RE: Chapter 1: Outline for Action

Since *Recruiting Love* is based on business principles, the tools will look much like the business tools you're already familiar with. Each chapter begins with a **15-Second Memo** which will give you the purpose of the chapter. At the end of each chapter you will find a **Summary Blueprint** and an **Action Memo**, which will be your personalized "to-do" list to keep you motivated, organized and on-track. **The Bottom Line** will encourage and inspire you to follow the tenets of the chapter.

Let's get started!

A "job search" for a special love is about to begin. You're the recruiter of the *You Company,* and a job is open for someone to be the lifetime partner. As the recruiter, you do the research to find, interview and select the perfect candidate and get that candidate to accept the position. You're in a unique position in this search, however, because you're not only the *recruiter* of the *You Company* — you *are* the *You Company!* Therefore, you are also the recruiter's client! In this role, you will thoroughly determine the needed qualifications, create a marketing plan for highlighting the *You Company's* assets and minimizing the liabilities, and make sure the search is producing qualified candidates.

In PART I: **The Research Process** (Chapters 1-3) you will ask yourself:

- ♥ Why does the "You Company" need to fill this job vacancy? (Why do you want to recruit love?)

- ♥ What is the precise job description? (What qualities are important to you, what qualities can you accept, and what qualities are out of the question?)

- ♥ What benefits and work environment is the "You Company" offering the right "candidate" (What assets and liabilities do YOU bring?)

In PART II: **The Recruiting Process** (Chapter 4) and PART III: **The Interview Process** (Chapters 5-7) you will use the information from PART I to do your targeting, marketing and interviewing. You will determine the best markets to advertise for your candidate, and market the *You Company* to those candidates. You'll also begin "interviewing" candidates, and we'll give you tools to change the way you think about dating!

In PART IV: **The Decision-Making Process** (Chapter 8) you will narrow down the search by re-evaluating all the information you have gathered in PARTS I, II and III. You'll make some adjustments to your recruiting plan and get new ideas to keep you motivated.

In PART V: **The Selection Process** (Chapter 9) we'll help you make decisions and resolve dilemmas about the candidates and the search process. You'll review legal and practical aspects to signing a "love contract." You'll see how to choose the best candidate from among the finalists, or how to adapt your plan if you've hit a delay. You'll also learn the best ways to start a new search if none of the candidates are right.

Finally, in Chapter 10, we'll leave you with some parting words of wisdom and ask you to file a voluntary report so we can help other recruiters learn from your success.

Now, before you begin, we have a few suggestions to help you:

- ♥ Get organized with a date book or calendar, or any time-management system (Filofax, Daytimer, etc.). This will remind you what you need to do, and keep you focused as you move through each step.

- ♥ Also get a small notebook to carry with you at all times. You will use this both for your initial research, and for your "dating log," as you interview candidates. (You'll be reading more on this unique dating tool in Chapter 4.)

- ♥ Carry this book with you, and refer to it frequently for support and guidance. (You never know; there could be that special someone on that crowded train following the same plan!)

16   Recruiting Love

- ♥ Most importantly, keep a positive outlook. Your goal IS attainable and you WILL achieve it!

> **Cheryl said:**
> I never had any trouble getting dates. After college I went to work for a great company. I thought I'd find my "prince" and have it all. As time went by, my job took more of my time and I didn't have as much time for a social life. Waiting for men to ask me out as I'd always done didn't work anymore. When I finally found a man I really liked, he turned out to be married. The next man I dated was also married. I got really discouraged, but then I met Ted, and I thought: "This is the one!"
>
> We were inseparable for three months, and I started thinking about our future together. After a romantic dinner, Ted said, "Cheryl, I have something important to tell you." I heard wedding bells! He looked into my eyes and said..."I can't lie to you anymore..I'm married with four children." Instead of pulling a ring box out of his pocket, he

In Real Life, the Toad Stays a Toad, and Then Keeps Calling!

> produced his kids' pictures. Every man I kiss turns into a toad instead of a prince. I need a plan!

Why Traditional Dating Methods Don't Work

In fairy tales when you kiss a toad, the toad becomes a handsome prince. In real life, when you kiss a toad, the toad stays a toad, and then keeps calling!

Whether you're male or female, odds are you've kissed a few toads. You had a plan to get your job, didn't you? Well, you need a plan to find love, too. Now that you're not a teenager anymore, or if you've been feeling like a "geek magnet" lately, you need a new strategy — one for adults. If your dates (or lack of) aren't working, keep reading, and keep an open mind.

Everyone knows dating at any age is challenging, but for adults it's especially hard. You have less time, more responsibilities, more expenses, and less energy. Most of us can no longer get by on just our looks, and the "pickins" are slimmer. Let's face it — meeting good people is not as easy as it used to be. It can be time consuming, sometimes dangerous, and you might not get as good a "rate of return" for your efforts. A couple of bad dates used to be no big deal — there was always another opportunity. But now, each disappointing date represents an investment of time you can't afford to lose.

Why don't your teenage dating methods work now?

- ♥ Time: When you were a teenager, you had school and maybe a part-time job and a few chores at home. Other than that, you were able to spend every minute on your social life. Now you have a demanding, responsible job, a house or apartment to maintain, meals to shop for and cook, etc. There's just no time to date every person you meet.

♥ Motivation: If you work all day (and some evenings and weekends!) and take care of your other responsibilities, you're probably more interested in lounging on your sofa than lounging at the "lounge."

♥ Fewer People: Many people have already teamed up. The remainder may have problems (fear of commitment, walking wounded, totally crazy, bad teeth?) All the good "fish in the sea" aren't taken, but the ocean's big and you have to cast a longer line to find them.

♥ Competition: The older you get, the more intense competition gets. The good news is that you're really not competing with younger or older people because usually there's little in common between vastly different age groups.

♥ Dignity: When you've had enough rejection, you think that there might be something wrong with you. If you find yourself hiding out at home with "Ben & Jerry" instead of dating another Tom, Dick or Mary, it isn't YOU: your dignity has been assaulted.

♥ Money: So, how many coffee dates do you really want to go on? Unless you're just having drinks, dating can get expensive (if you're a single parent...a lot more expensive). Since men and women usually share expenses, modern dating is going to take a bite out of your wallet.

♥ Danger: Let's face it, the era of "free love" is over. If you ignore this, you may end up paying with your life. Today, AIDS, date rape and other "cheerful aspects" of socializing are a sad, but very real part of dating.

Nobody finds love without kissing a few toads along the way, but dating doesn't have to be a "bummer." If you follow the steps in *Recruiting Love*, you'll get to your goal faster, you'll feel good about what you're doing, and you'll have fun while you're looking too. (Starting with this book!)

Put your past behind you, and throw out your old ideas about dating.

Repeat after us: "I've had my last bad date; I'm going to find my ideal mate."

Relax. You can do this!

Think Before You Act

Many single adults feel like they've lost control of their social lives. If you feel that way, you can get it back! Just as you made decisions about your career – what were you going to do, what skills/education you needed, etc. – you can (and must) take charge of how you search for love.

First, imagine yourself as the boss of your own company. You're looking for a special person to be your partner. You're going to recruit that person by using the same business skills that you've already used in the world of work. This will give you the focus you need. We're also going to give you some special charts and action memos to track your progress. You are **not** a helpless victim! You are in control.

Unless you were very lucky, or had a family business, before you entered the workforce you had to look for a job. If it has been a long time since you last job-hunted, or you've never looked for a job in the traditional way, we're going to review the process that most people go through to find a job.

Think back about your initial motivation for finding a job. Maybe you needed extra money to pay for school. Later on, it might have been to get some experience in your field. As you continued along your career path you probably looked for jobs for a variety of reasons such as more responsibility, higher salary, layoffs, etc. In any case, you knew why you wanted to find a job and what type of job you would like to have.

You have to think before you act — you can't just apply for everything you come across and hope you'll get the job you want. You carefully research the job market and see where you best fit in. You prepare your resume to emphasize your strengths and minimize your weaknesses. You select the jobs that match your qualifications, and that most closely meet your needs. Hopefully, if you've done your homework, you'll get a call for an interview.

A job interview makes most people anxious; you never know exactly how it will turn out. But even if it doesn't turn out as you hoped, you know that it only takes one good interview to find the right job.

In order to land a job, you must also prepare yourself for the interview. You learn all you can about your prospective employer. You gather your optimism, select an appropriate outfit, prepare answers to tough questions, and psych yourself up to go to the interview (on time, of course).

The job interview is an exchange of information. Ideally it works both ways, with the interviewer learning about you, and you learning about the company. Sometimes, the job isn't what you thought, or there just isn't any chemistry. Sometimes you'd really like the job, but the interviewer doesn't think you're right for it. Sometimes the interviewer likes you but you don't like the job. There are many reasons why an interview may or may not work out, but you should always make the best impression you can. No matter what the outcome (even if you can't wait for it to end) if you impress the interviewer it might ultimately lead to something better.

And landing the job doesn't end there!

You also have to follow up with the employer, even if you're not sure you want the job. Then you wait — there might be more interviews before you get the job you want. Suppose everything went well and you get an offer. Of course you'd try to negotiate the best terms, but you might not get everything you want. If the whole package seems good, you'll accept (after all, nothing's perfect). Then, you'll share your good news with everyone, and file away your job hunting materials.

The job hunting process has ended. Now, you will be expected to work hard and live up to the qualifications for which you were selected over all the other candidates. This will occur most naturally if your new job relies on your strengths, doesn't weigh too heavily on your weaknesses, and you are comfortable with the company's environment and philosophy.

The search for love works the same way!

In *Recruiting Love*, you have to do your research before you put yourself out there. If you skip this step you may end up like Cheryl — with a string of married boyfriends instead of a committed relationship. You have to know what you want, why you want it, and where to go looking for it. You also have to list your strengths and weaknesses. You will keep all of this in mind throughout your search, using it to locate the types of people you want to meet. Just like the job seeker sends out résumés, you also have to let people know you're available and market yourself in the best possible way. If you've done your up-front work thoughtfully and thoroughly, you'll begin to arrange interviews with possible candidates (dates).

Just as for a job interview, you have to prepare yourself for a love recruitment interview. You'll gather your optimism and learn all you can about your candidate beforehand, dress to impress, think of witty ice-breakers, and psyche yourself up to meet at the appointed place (on time, of course).

As you talk to each other to find out if there's a match, either of you may realize that there isn't one. Don't take it personally. Perhaps you or your candidate had a bad day and might have been more receptive some other time. It's still best to make a good impression because just like in a job interview, even if the love interview doesn't work out, it may lead to something else.

If your candidate calls to ask you out again (or if you call, and s/he accepts) sooner or later you'll have to negotiate the terms of the relationship. Will it be friendship, lovers, or even marriage? That's up to both of you. Just like a job offer, there may be qualities you don't like (less-than-fabulous looking, too many roommates, etc.). However, if the total package seems like a good deal, you'll accept. Then you'll share the good news with everyone and file away your love seeking materials.

And, of course, both of you will want to work hard to maintain the relationship as the great match you always wanted. If you've selected wisely, you'll be glad every day of your life that you had the intelligence and courage to make a plan, go through the effort, and make the right choice.

courage to make a plan, go through the effort, and make the right choice.

If you're thinking that this whole process isn't very romantic, you're right. It may seem more romantic for fate to bring you the person you really want, but the reality is that it's terribly UNromantic to end up with unplanned dates that turn out badly. Despite what you read in the "Prince Charming" stories as a child, we haven't found many couples who had fairy tale romances. Good relationships take a lot of work and planning; they don't just happen.

Don't skip any of the steps in *Recruiting Love*. Each chapter has been designed to build on the one before.

We've designed some special tools to keep you organized and motivated. **15-Second Memos** start each chapter to tell you what lies ahead; **The Bottom Line** ends each chapter with a saying to motivate you and remind you of the chapter's main focus; **Summary Blueprints** drive home the main points. We've also developed unique **Action Memos** (**TO DO** lists) for each chapter to copy and carry with you.

───────── THE BOTTOM LINE ─────────
"When we look around us at the modern world, we see business everywhere, unless of course we happen to be, for example, in the bathroom." Dave Barry

From the desk of: The Advice Sisters

TO: *You Company* Recruiter

FROM: Alison and Jessica

RE: Summary of Chapter 1: Outline for Action

1. Traditional dating methods don't work well for adults because of:
   - Lack of time and motivation
   - Fewer people to choose from
   - Ego damage
   - Cost of dating
   - Potential dangers

2. As an adult, you must take control of your love search. You must:
   - Have a plan
   - Consider yourself the "boss" of your own company (and the "You Company" recruiter).
   - Use familiar job search skills to recruit love.

3. Summary of Job Hunting/Love Hunting Skills:
   - Prepare: think before you act
   - Assess: your strengths and weaknesses
   - Research: market to see where you fit in
   - Target: places/people you want to reach
   - Gather: information for your interview/date
   - Interviews/dates are exchanges of information.
   - Landing the job/mate doesn't end with the interview/date...negotiate.

4. Each chapter builds on the others, so don't skip any!

From the desk of: The Advice Sisters

Today's Date: _____

1. If you haven't already done so, get a datebook, a binder/Filofax etc., and a small spiral notebook. These tools will help to keep your search organized.

   I will complete this by: _____

2. Do a self affirmation. Say to yourself: "I'm going to recruit love: I've had my last bad date." Write it on a sticky note and put it on your bathroom mirror.

   I will complete this by: _____

3. Go on to Chapter 2.

   I will complete this by: _____

Action Memo

Successful Single
1111 Happiness Way
Anytown, USA 99999-1111

Objective
To apply my interviewing and organization skills to a sweeter purpose – finding love!

Personal Information
Enjoy canoeing, whitewater rafting, sailboating - anything outdoors! Looking for partner to share the great outdoors, possibly leading to marriage.

Assets
Good sense of humor, good listener, generous

Potential Liabilities
Vegetarian -- no dates at the steak house. Like to wake up at the crack of dawn, even on weekends and holidays.

Experience
Most recent previous relationship approximately six months -- wanted family right away; I'd like to wait about five more years.

A few dates before that, but haven't been able to connect with anyone who shares my love of outdoor activities.

From the desk of: The Advice Sisters

TO: *You Company* Recruiter

FROM: Alison and Jessica

RE: Chapter 2: Drafting the *You Company Candidate Job Description* (Who Do You Really Want to Hire?)

In *Recruiting Love*, you are the love-recruiter for the *You Company*, and only you can determine what qualities the ideal candidate:

- ♥ Absolutely must have
- ♥ Should optimally have
- ♥ Cannot have at all (qualities you will not accept under any circumstances).

In this chapter we'll take you through some investigative exercises to help you clarify and expand what the *You Company* really wants.

Read this chapter even if you believe that you already know what you're looking for. If you can easily and thoroughly answer all of the questions in the *You Company Job Description Worksheet*, complete the *You Company Candidate Job Description* and move ahead to Chapter 3.

If you feel it's necessary to investigate your candidate qualities further, look into other resources (we'll suggest some) before you move on.

15-Second Memo

When an executive recruiter recruits for a position, s/he first reviews the client's written job description and then says: *"I see what the job description says you want. Now, what I do I **really** need to know about the job and your requirements to find the right candidate?"*

In order for the recruiter to find the right candidate, the client must be honest and precise about what qualities the candidate **must** have and what qualities are **unacceptable**.

You've probably already thought about what you want in a partner. You may want to skip this step and immediately begin recruiting. We urge you not to do this, because no matter how clear you think your vision is, it may still be incomplete. A savvy executive would never expend company time and money on a long-term project without careful planning. *Recruiting Love* works the same way. If you don't take the time to list your needs, you will cheat the *You Company* out of your own valuable time and resources.

> ▶ Mary said:
> You could say that I'd been around the dating scene long enough to qualify me as an expert. I'd been divorced for more than ten years and I definitely kissed my share of toads. I began reading *Recruiting Love* because I had grown weary of the same old places to meet singles, and I needed a better plan to find someone special. Chapter 1 made me so excited about beginning my search that I wanted to skip the "boring investigative stuff." I'd been searching for a long time and I knew what I wanted. Fortunately, I read through Chapters 2 and 3 anyway, without completing any of the

> investigative exercises. I was amazed when I was stumped on the very first question (about my relationship goal)! I could easily answer some questions, but there were others that I'd never even thought about. My vision of an ideal mate wasn't clear or complete at all. Putting my vision on paper showed dating patterns I never knew I had. Eventually, my research led me to Bradley — my ideal candidate!

Creating The Job Description

When a position becomes available (especially if the position is new) the employer must first consider the purpose of the job and why it should be filled. S/he must also decide what qualifications the ideal candidate must have. All of this is translated into a job description. We are going to go through the same process for you to create the *You Company Job Description.*

As the employer and the recruiter of the *You Company,* you too must first decide why you want someone to fill the position of loving you. In other words, why do you want to recruit love? You must *also* consider what kind of person you want, and what his/her qualifications must be.

We'll ask you some thought-provoking questions. After each question, mark your answer on the *You Company Job Description Worksheet* beginning on page 44. After you complete these exercises, you will fill in the *You Company Job Description Form,* which will be an essential part of your search and selection process!

Now let's begin with the most essential question:

?

1. Why do I want to recruit love?

- ❏ Companionship
- ❏ To fill an emotional void
- ❏ Marriage
- ❏ Family pressures
- ❏ A family
- ❏ Sex
- ❏ Social acceptance
- ❏ A mom/dad for my kids
- ❏ Financial security
- ❏ Other: _____

If you have more than one reason, number them in order of priority. Now write your answers in at (1) on the *You Company Job Description Worksheet.*

If you had trouble clarifying your goals, you should consider whether you are ready for a relationship, or if there may be other reasons that you're looking for a partner. Consider these statements:

a. I am ready to share my life with someone.

b. The rest of my life is pretty much the way I want it.

c. I am willing to overcome any obstacles to finding love.

d. I am willing to be flexible in my new relationships.

e. I am willing to risk my feelings to find love.

f. I am eager to become a parent.

g. Finding a partner is on top of my list of priorities.

h. I am emotionally secure.

i. I'm nothing without a partner.

j. No one good would ever want me.

k. I'm left out because I'm the only one of my group who is not married.

l. My biological clock is ticking and it's driving me crazy.

m. My family expects me to get married and have kids.

n. I'm not sure I want love, but I do want sex.

Which, if any, of these statements did you identify with? Statements A-H indicate that you're ready to have a love relationship, and are probably seeking companionship, marriage and/or a family. If you identify more strongly with statements J-N, you may have other reasons for recruiting love. If you identify with both groups, it may be a signal that you have conflicting feelings about recruiting love. People connect for a variety of reasons. Our book isn't meant to delve deeply into your psyche, but take note: if you aren't clear about your real needs and motivations, you must now define what your search is really about. This is important to stay focused and motivated. If you need to, do some research by talking to friends, family members, a therapist, counselor, mentor, advisor, religious leader, etc. Reflect upon your past relationships to help you sort out what you want now.

> Doug said:
> I'd had several serious relationships, and I'd even lived with a woman for a while. I think I was in love with her, but although both our families expected us to get married, I just couldn't commit. I dated lots of other interesting women, but I always started to "cool" as soon as things started getting serious. I couldn't understand why I couldn't get past my fear of commitment — especially since the women I dated were great — even my friends and family thought so!
> Then I met Elisabeth and brought her home for the holidays, as I'd done with a number of other women. The minute my folks met Elisabeth, they instantly fell in love with her. The problem was, once they liked her, I began liking her less. It wasn't anything she said or did; I just became

turned off. Eventually, we split up. I think my Mom and Dad were more upset than either of us!

One of the investigative exercises in the recruiting love plan was to write down all of your past relationships, and the primary reasons for their breakups. There was a distinct pattern. I really did love many of the women that I had dated; however, the minute I would think seriously about them my passion would cool. This would always happen after bringing the woman home to meet my folks.

I quickly realized what was going on. The minute I started getting serious with someone, my folks started "mentally" planning the wedding. I felt pressure to get married to please them. I recalled that after one dinner with Elisabeth, Mom told me that we had a great aunt named Elisabeth and that it would be great if we named our first child after her. First child! We had just started going steady, and weren't even talking about get engaged! Mom had skipped right over the wedding and went directly to the grandchildren!

When I finished the recruiting love exercises, I had a serious talk with my folks about this problem and, believe it or not, they didn't even realize what they were doing.

I'm dating someone special again, but this time, I know that the decision to make our relationship permanent is mine and mine alone.

Look at Your Past To Go Forward

When a client wishes to fill an available position s/he looks at who has filled the job before, and what assets and liabilities that person had. Has anyone loved you before? If so, what assets and liabilities have attracted and repelled you? From the following list, check off those which you NOW consider "must haves" in a candidate, those which are "negotiable/optional" and those which are totally unacceptable. Don't settle out of desperation, or because you're tired of searching. Keep in mind, though, the more requirements you insist upon, the more difficult it may be to find and hire that special candidate.

Now, select the top six assets and liabilities in order of priority and note them on the worksheet under (2a) on page 42.

ASSETS	LIABILITIES
good looks	unattractive
sense of humor	solemn
generous	greedy/cheap
good communicator/listener	uncommunicative
self-esteem	low self-esteem
healthy (mental/physical)	mental/physical problems
financially secure	money problems
does/doesn't have children	does/doesn't have children
wants/doesn't want children	wants/doesn't want children
geographically desirable	geographically undesirable

Creating the Job Description 35

sexually compatible	sexually incompatible
adaptable	rigid
no substance abuse	addict
smoker/nonsmoker	smoker/nonsmoker
enthusiastic about me	ambivalent about me
sociable	unfriendly
family likes me	family is unaccepting
friends are accepting	friends are unaccepting
sensitive	insensitive
caring	cold
honest	dishonest
not afraid of commitment	commitment-phoebe
industrious	lazy
loyal	disloyal
compassionate	unsympathetic
available	unavailable
romantic	unromantic
interesting	boring
intelligent	stupid
similar educations	different educations
shares feelings	closed

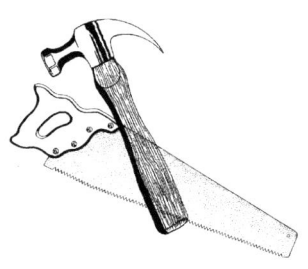

similar interests/values	different interests/values
even-tempered	bad-tempered
giver	taker/user
self assured	boastful/bragging
trusting	jealous
cooperative	overly competitive
other (list):	other (list):
_____	_____
_____	_____

Now think back to any past relationships. On a separate piece of paper, list each of them by name. Describe in one sentence how and why each relationship ended. Now, refer to the above list, and select the six most significant assets and the six most significant liabilities of your past partners. Note them at (2b) on page 42.

Can you see any patterns? Were all of them unavailable? Were many of them romantic? Were a majority bad-tempered? Did most of your past partners have a good sense of humor?

Take another look at the assets and liabilities you determined were important in your future candidates. Which assets and liabilities are the same as those of your past partners, and which ones are different? Thinking about what has or hasn't worked in the past will help you make better choices in your future relationships.

Consider "Job Histories"

Your candidates also have past histories, and you'll want to consider their "past performance" in love. The following exercise will help you zero in on potential problem spots to consider when creating your candidate job description.

Enter your responses at (3).

- ♥ What other relationships has your candidate had in the past?
- ♥ What level of commitment was involved?
- ♥ What caused the relationship(s) to break up?
- ♥ Is there anything in a candidates' past that might signal trouble? (e.g. substance abuse, physical abuse, criminal record, bankruptcy, mental/physical/health problems, inability to keep a job, rocky family relationships, political/religious, physical characteristics, fanaticism, opportunist, sexual perversions, etc.)

How about your personal compatibility with a candidate? First, rate the importance of the following traits using any scale you'd like:

eating/sleeping habits

fitness habits

world/life outlook

personal hygiene

personal expression

ambition

work habits

self-image

sexual style and interest level

willingness to make changes

hobbies and outside interests

manners/social behavior

attitude towards work/fun

handling stress

religious beliefs

handling setbacks

same race

relationship goals

physical characteristics

personality traits

others (list):

At (4a) on page 43, list any traits which both you and your candidate must have in order to be compatible. At (4b) list any traits that might cause you to reject an otherwise viable candidate.

Finally, think about any other important factors in selecting a candidate (pet lover/hates animals, drinker/teatoatler, loves/hates dancing, etc.) and list them at (5).

Since most adults have been thinking about these issues for some time, it should not have been difficult to answer the questions. However, if you did have a hard time, and you don't feel comfortable with your answers, you may need to clarify your needs. You may want to talk to a friend, a counselor, or anyone else that you trust.

Creating the Candidate Job Description

Now that you have filled in the *You Company Job Description Worksheet,* you have determined your ideal candidate's most important qualities. Using this information, fill in the *You Company Job Description Form* on page 44. This form will serve as an official job description for your ideal candidate, which you will be using throughout the recruitment process.

Congratulations! You are now almost half-way done with your initial assessments. In the next chapter we will help you create the *You Company Profile,* which will pinpoint your assets and liabilities.

THE BOTTOM LINE

"The only thing which is not purely mechanical about falling in love is its beginning. Although all those who fall in love do so in the same way, not all fall in love for the same reason. There is no single quality which is universally loved." Jose Ortega y Gasset

From the desk of: The Advice Sisters

Summary Blueprint

TO: *You Company* Recruiter

FROM: Alison and Jessica

RE: Summary of Chapter 3: Creating the *You Company Profile* (Assessing Yourself)

1. The *You Company Profile* is a tool to help you attract good candidates, and to convince the right candidate that the *You Company* is the best choice!

2. Your *You Company Profile* reminds you of your assets throughout the search, and reminds you of any liabilities which might cause trouble during or after your search.

3. If you have difficulty identifying your goals, strengths and weaknesses, use other resources to help you.

From the desk of: The Advice Sisters

Today's Date: _____

1. Complete the exercises in Chapter 3, and complete the *You Company Profile*.

I will complete this by: _____

2. Great! You feel confident that the information is accurate. Go to Chapter 4.

I will complete this by: _____

3. You're not totally confident about your *You Company Profile*. Clarify your personal strengths and possible liabilities, seeking other resources to help you if necessary. Then go on to Chapter 4.

I will complete this by: _____

Action Memo

You Company Candidate Job Description
WORKSHEET

1. My relationship objective(s) is/are: _____

   _____

2a. These assets and liabilities are most important to me in a candidate now:

ASSETS	LIABILITIES
1. _____	1. _____
2. _____	2. _____
3. _____	3. _____
4. _____	4. _____
5. _____	5. _____
6. _____	6. _____

2b. These assets and liabilities were most important (and prevalent) in my past partners:

ASSETS	LIABILITIES
1. _____	1. _____
2. _____	2. _____
3. _____	3. _____
4. _____	4. _____
5. _____	5. _____
6. _____	6. _____

3. Here are some potential problem spots to watch for in my candidate assessment:

_____

_____

_____

4a. I want my ideal candidate to have these personal traits similar to mine:

_____

_____

_____

4b. These are traits that might cause me to reject an otherwise viable candidate:

_____

_____

_____

5. Here are other characteristics that are particularly important to me:

_____

_____

_____

You Company Candidate Job Description

For _____ 's love search.
         (your name)

I am seeking a candidate to fill the job of (write your relationship objectives):

_____

_____

The basic requirements for the position are (top six assets):

1. _____ 4. _____
2. _____ 5. _____
3. _____ 6. _____

My ideal candidate must also have (six next most important assets):

1. _____ 4. _____
2. _____ 5. _____
3. _____ 6. _____

If possible, my candidate should also have the following (List the optional assets you have chosen):

_____

_____

_____

Creating the Job Description 45

Other pluses would include (list any special qualifications you have chosen):

_____
_____
_____

NO candidates with the following need apply (list any negatives/liabilities):

_____
_____
_____

But I will consider candidates who meet the basic requirements even if (list negotiable liabilities):

_____
_____
_____

I expect to hire a candidate by: _____

(target date)

Why would he date me? I'm so plain and fat!

From the desk of: The Advice Sisters

TO: *You Company* Recruiter

FROM: Alison and Jessica

RE: Chapter 3: Creating the *You Company Profile* (Assessing Yourself)

In order to get good candidates to apply, and to convince the right one that the *You Company* is the right place, you need to effectively "sell" the company. In this chapter we will help you create the *You Company Profile*, which will pinpoint your assets and identify your liabilities.

Read this chapter even if you believe you already know what the *You Company* is all about. If you can easily and thoroughly answer all the questions in the chapter, complete the *You Company Profile* and move ahead to Chapter 4. On the other hand, if you feel it's necessary for you to appraise the *You Company* further, look into other resources before you go on.

In Chapter 2, you assessed what the *You Company* was looking for in a candidate. You wrote a "job description" to identify those qualities and traits you want for your special someone.

But it's not enough just to locate the candidate you want — that person has to accept the job. In business, a recruiter must "sell the company" to the applicant by talking about the benefits (e.g. great work environment, advancement potential) while playing down the negatives (e.g. poor health plan, long hours).

So, what does the *You Company* have to offer? In this chapter you'll answer this question by assessing yourself, and creating a *You Company Profile* (your own assets) to "sell the company."

Perhaps in a job interview, you've heard: "Tell me about yourself." What did you say? You probably talked about your skills, work experience, goals and interests — maybe your expectations for the job. You probably didn't talk about your personal values, your deepest feelings, or any overly personal information not relevant to the job search. But a love search requires different information about yourself and what you have to offer. This takes a lot of thought, because it's harder to square your concept of yourself with how others perceive you.

As we did in Chapter 2, we'll provide some investigative exercises to help you create the *You Company Profile*. The *You Company* may not want to broadcast any liabilities, but it's important for you to know what they are so that you can either correct them or be aware of how they may affect your search.

▶ Mike's story:

Mike was an avid reader of self-help books, had gone through the EST program in the '70s, and had even made a pilgrimage to India to seek spiritual guidance from a famous Maharishi. By the time he began the *Recruiting Love* plan, he insisted that there was no need for him to do any more personal investigation. We urged him to complete his personal profile, and he humored us. According to Mike, he had many assets, but only one liability — he was a big talker. Now he simply needed to ask his friends a few questions about himself — how hard could that be?

Mike was shocked when he learned that his friends' perceptions of him didn't concur with his own. His friends never mentioned that he talked too much. Instead, they told him that while he was a loyal friend, he was arrogant and pushy around women. They suggested that instead of picking weak partners and then putting them down for being intellectually inferior, he might be happier with women who were more of a challenge.

Armed with this knowledge, he was not only able to promote his "company" more positively, he also began selecting women who better matched his personality and intelligence. "I thought I knew everything there was to know about myself," said Mike, "but even after all that self-knowledge stuff, I was still blind to my own faults. I'm grateful that my friends had the courage to tell me that I could make some changes. If I'd recruited candidates without their insight, I never would have selected Linda, and I would never have gotten her to accept my "job offer."

Answer the following questions, and mark your final conclusions on the *You Company Profile* form at the end of the chapter. Once you've completed this form, you will have a complete *You Company Profile* to refer to throughout your search.

1. You have so many facets. Some you can see, and some you can't. Let's begin with what's on the outside — your physical attributes and personal data. How do you view yourself? How do others view you?

I would consider my height to be:
- ❏ Short
- ❏ Average
- ❏ Tall

I would consider my weight as:
- ❏ Underweight
- ❏ Average
- ❏ Overweight

My age is: _____

My current hair color is: _____

I would consider my health to be:

- ❏ Excellent
- ❏ Good
- ❏ Fair
- ❏ Poor

I would consider my fitness level to be:

- ❏ Excellent
- ❏ Good
- ❏ Fair
- ❏ Poor

The thing(s) I like best about my looks is/are:

_____

_____

My most unique physical feature is:

_____

_____

The thing(s) I'd like to change if I could about my looks is/are:

_____

_____

Generally speaking, I would describe my appearance as:
- ☐ Gorgeous
- ☐ Attractive
- ☐ Average
- ☐ Could use some work

Most people would say that my appearance is:
- ☐ Gorgeous
- ☐ Attractive
- ☐ Average
- ☐ Could use some work

My current marital status is: _____

I have been:
- ☐ Married _____ times
- ☐ Divorced _____ times
- ☐ Widowed _____ times.
- ☐ Never married
- ☐ Lived together _____ times
- ☐ Monogamous relationship _____ times
- ☐ I've never had a serious relationship

Now place your answers at (1) on the *You Company Profile* form.

In Chapter 2, you examined your past relationships to determine what you consider to be assets and liabilities in a partner. Now it's time to consider your own assets and liabilities using the same list. Put a "*" next to your assets, and an "x" next to the liabilities.

<u>ASSETS</u>
good looks
sense of humor
generous
good communicator/listener
self-esteem
healthy (mental/physical)
financially secure

<u>LIABILITIES</u>
unattractive
solemn
greedy/cheap
uncommunicative
low self-esteem
mental/physical problems
money problems

have/don't have children
want/don't want children
geographically desirable
adaptable
no substance abuse
smoker/nonsmoker
sociable

have/don't have children
want/don't want children
geographically undesirable
rigid
addict
smoker/nonsmoker
unfriendly

54 Recruiting Love

family is accepting   family is unaccepting

friends are accepting	friends are unaccepting
sensitive	insensitive
caring	cold
honest	dishonest
not afraid of commitment	commitment-phoebe
industrious	lazy
loyal	disloyal
compassionate	unsympathetic
available	unavailable
romantic	unromantic
interesting	boring
intelligent	stupid
share feelings	closed
happy	depressed
even-tempered	bad-tempered
giver	taker/user
self assured	boastful/bragging
trusting	jealous
cooperative	overly competitive
other (list more below)	other (list more below)

_____   _____

_____   _____

_____   _____

2a. Review the list and select your six most significant assets and your six most significant liabilities.

2b. Do you see anything you'd like to change?

3a. Now, select your next six most significant assets and liabilities. Double star "**" or double "xx" them.

3b. Do you see anything you'd like to change?

You've probably heard the expression: "one person's meat is another one's poison." What you consider to be your biggest asset or liability may not appear that way to everyone.

> Ursula said:
> I'm someone that people would call beautiful. It's true that I'm good looking, and I guess that I am lucky for it. I've been able to make a career doing fashion layouts and commercials. But in my opinion I'm too tall, too thin, and all arms and legs. In high school I couldn't even get a date. It's difficult to deal with the way some people look at me, and I hate to get unsolicited comments about my looks. That makes me feel uncomfortable.
>
> I get asked out a lot by men I think I might want to get to know better. Unfortunately, I often find that they haven't asked me out because of who I am, or what I think, but because of how I look. I'm interested in finding a man who wants to date all of me — not just my body!
>
> When I did my personal profile, I listed my looks as one of my primary liabilities. Some people cannot understand how I could possibly think this way. After all, isn't beauty supposed to be a woman's best asset? Well, from my standpoint,

> my looks have kept me from making relationships with men, and have contributed to my being shy and withdrawn. My looks should be an asset, but to me, they're just a liability.

Your past relationships are also very important to your personal profile, and will help guide you as you select future candidates. On a separate piece of paper, write the name of each person. Under each name answer the following questions:

- ♥ What level of commitment was involved?
- ♥ What caused the relationship(s) to break up?
- ♥ Do you see any patterns in your choices or in the ways things ended?

4a. Go over your past love information and list the major reasons for the breakups.

4b. If you see any patterns, list them under (4b).

5. Is there anything in your past that might signal trouble for your relationship (substance abuse, physical abuse, criminal record, bankruptcy, mental/physical/health problems, inability to keep a job, rocky family relationships, political/religious, physical characteristics, fanaticism, opportunist, sexual perversions, addictions, etc?) Mark any trouble spots at (5).

6. From the following list, select any traits of yours which might cause problems in a future relationship:

attitude towards ambition

attitude towards work/fun

attitude towards family/friends

eating/sleeping habits

fitness habits

world/life outlook

personal hygiene

personal expression

ambition

work habits

self-image

sexual style and interest level

willingness to make changes

hobbies and outside interests

manners/social behavior

handling stress

religious beliefs

handling setbacks

problem-solving style

relationship goals

physical characteristics

other:

7. Is there anything else about yourself that you think might be important to your candidate (keep pythons as pets, sleepwalker etc.).

We've asked to you consider your physical attributes and your character/personality traits, but how about your feelings about your love search? You don't have to list these answerson the *You Company Profile*. Just take a moment and consider how you're feeling about your search for love:

1. The thing(s) I'm most excited about in starting a new relationship is/are:

   _____

   _____

2. The thing(s) I'm most apprehensive about in starting a new relationship is/are:

   _____

   _____

3. The easiest thing(s) to do in recruiting love is/are:

   _____

   _____

4. The hardest thing(s) to do in recruiting love is/are:

   _____

   _____

5. I will gain more from a new relationship than I will lose.

   ___Yes   ___No

We've just found out how you perceive yourself, but how do other people perceive you? Those who are close to you can provide some clues, as Mike discovered to his surprise. Ask your closest friend(s) these questions, and enter the answers on the *You Company Profile* form on page 67.

8a. What do you think are my three best qualities?

8b. You would describe my personality as:

8c. If you were going to pick one thing about me that you think I should change, it would be:

8d. One piece of advice you'd give me about my love search is:

8e. You'd describe my last partner as:

8f. If you were the recruiter for my next partner, you'd select someone who:

Look at your friend(s) responses. Is there a pattern? If so, have you overlooked anything in your assessment?

As we've said before, we assume that you're reading *Recruiting Love* because you really **want** to be in a serious, love relationship. Before you go on, look at this list of reasons people have given us for not wanting a relationship. Do any of these apply to you?

- ♥ There's no one "out there" for me.
- ♥ I'm basically a loner.
- ♥ I'm scared of commitment.
- ♥ I don't want to be responsible for anyone else.
- ♥ I don't want to rely on anyone else.

- ♥ My work is my life.
- ♥ I have no time to look for love.
- ♥ I live my way and I won't change for anyone.
- ♥ I don't want to move, or have someone move in.
- ♥ I'm a geek magnet.
- ♥ I don't know what a good relationship is.
- ♥ I'm not lucky.
- ♥ Relationships suffocate me.
- ♥ I'm focusing on me; there's no time for anyone else.
- ♥ I hate sex.
- ♥ Everyone I know in a relationship is unhappy.
- ♥ I hate dating.
- ♥ No one good would want me.
- ♥ Men/women can't be trusted.
- ♥ I don't want to get hurt.
- ♥ What if I eventually find someone better out there?

Did any of these statements apply to you? If so, remember that your work doesn't end once you've selected a candidate and s/he has selected you. To KEEP the relationship for a lifetime, you'll need to commit to it every day — just as you're doing now.

As we've said before, *Recruiting Love* isn't a psychology book, but we can say that any of these statements can just be manifestations of anxiety. If you lack self-confidence, you may cover your fear of rejection with statements like: "I'm not lucky," "I'm a geek magnet," or "There's no one out there for me."

If you've gone through a breakup you may say things like: "Everyone I know in a relationship is unhappy," "Men/women can't be trusted," or, "I'm not lucky."

If you've been single for a long time, you might say: "My work is my life," "I don't want to move, or have someone move in," or "I live my way and I won't change for anyone."

It takes two to commit, so be sure you really want to recruit and keep your love before you continue!

Now that you've filled in all the blanks on the worksheet, you have a composite description of the *You Company.* Congratulations — you've completed all the assessments you need to begin your search!

The exercises are designed to help you investigate your assets and liabilities, as well as to see how you appear to others. If you had difficulty, you may want to think more about your personal attributes. Consider talking with friends, relatives or a therapist.

===== THE BOTTOM LINE =====

"Know thyself." On the wall at the Oracle at Delphi

From the desk of: The Advice Sisters

TO: *You Company* Recruiter

FROM: Alison and Jessica

RE: Summary of Chapter 2: Drafting the *You Company* Job Description (Who Do You Really Want to Recruit?)

1. As both recruiter and employer/client for the *You Company*, you must decide what qualities the ideal candidate must have, which qualities are optional, and which qualities are unacceptable.

2. The *You Company* candidate job description will keep you focused during your search. It may be revised or adjusted during the recruitment and search process.

3. If the investigative exercises are difficult for you, perhaps you need extra time to clarify your needs. Take advantage of other resources if you need to.

Summary Blueprint

From the desk of: The Advice Sisters

Today's Date: _____

1. Complete the exercises in Chapter 2, and create the *You Company Candidate Job Description Form.*

I will complete this by: _____

2. You are confident that the candidate job description you created is accurate. Go to Chapter 3.

I will complete this by: _____

3. You're not totally confident about the candidate job description. Clarify your needs, using other resources if necessary. Then go to Chapter 3.

I will complete this by: _____

Action Memo

You Company Profile

For _____ 's love search.

(your name)

Physical Attributes and Personal Data

Height: _____   Weight: _____

Age: _____   Hair color: _____

Health: _____   Fitness Level: _____

The thing(s) I like best about my looks is/are:

_____

_____

My most unique physical feature is: _____

The thing(s) I'd change (if I could) about how I look is/are:

_____

_____

Generally speaking, I would describe my looks as:

_____

Most people would say my looks are:

_____

My current marital status is: _____

I have been: (list as many as apply to you)

_____

_____

_____

My Personal Assets and Liabilities:

2a.   My six most important assets and liabilities are:

ASSETS	LIABILITIES
1. _____	1. _____
2. _____	2. _____
3. _____	3. _____
4. _____	4. _____
5. _____	5. _____
6. _____	6. _____

2b.   Some things I might like to change about myself are:

_____

_____

3a.   My six next important assets and liabilities are:

ASSETS	LIABILITIES
1. _____	1. _____
2. _____	2. _____
3. _____	3. _____
4. _____	4. _____
5. _____	5. _____
6. _____	6. _____

3b. Some things I might like to change about myself are:

_____

_____

4a. Reasons for breakups of my other relationships were:

_____

_____

4b. Patterns I see that I might want to think about are:

_____

_____

5. In my own personal history, I'll want to be aware of:

_____

_____

6. Other personal traits to be aware of are:

_____

_____

7. Other personal traits of mine that might be important factors to my candidates is/are:

_____

_____

How Others Perceive Me:

8a. Others think my best qualities are:

_____

_____

8b. Others would describe my personality as:

_____

_____

8c. Others think that one thing I might want to change about myself is:

_____

_____

8d. Others advice about my love search is:

_____

_____

8e. Others describe my last partner as:

_____

_____

8f. Others would choose for my next partner:

_____

_____

You're from Transylvania and I'm from Pennsylvania! Is this a small world or what?

From the desk of: The Advice Sisters

TO: *You Company* Recruiter

FROM: Alison and Jessica

RE: Chapter 4: Targeting the *You Company* Search (Pinpointing Specific Locales)

So far, you've made the decision to recruit love, determined the *You Company's* relationship goals and the qualifications for the ideal candidate. You have also developed a profile of the *You Company*. Now it's time to decide what type of candidate suits the *You Company* best. Then, you'll begin to recruit qualified people.

This chapter will help you find the **right** candidates in the **best** places. You'll also learn how to use a unique tool — the dating log — to manage your search.

15-Second Memo

Networking for Love

In business, successful people join professional organizations where they can socialize and network with like-minded individuals. They know it's an opportunity to expand their circle of contacts, and meet others who may help them in the future. Your love search works the same way. Tell people you trust about your search. Show them your personal profile, and you never know – they may suggest new candidates, or at least give you some valuable pointers.

What's Your "Approachability" Level?

Soon you will investigate the specific locales to recruit candidates, and enter the social scene for the first time as a love recruiter. Before you start, think for a moment about your overall "approachability" level. How easy are you to get to know? Do people naturally gravitate to you, or do they have to "warm up to you" before they feel comfortable?

Obviously, if you're highly approachable, recruiting will be much easier. However, some love recruiters are naturally shy and withdrawn. If this applies to you, upping your approachability level will boost your effectiveness. It's not as hard as you think! Practice a warm smile and a direct gaze, and you'll soon find that you're getting smiled at and talked to by people you've never met before. It takes fewer muscles to smile than to frown! So the next time someone on line at the bank makes a comment about the weather, don't just ignore it. Maybe s/he's just passing the time while waiting for a teller, but then again, maybe this person is attracted to you. You're stuck on line anyway so why not smile and answer back? Practice being open and outgoing wherever you go. You never know – the supermarket shopper you asked about cooking eggplant might just turn out to be your perfect candidate!

Targeting your Search

Now that you're open to meeting people everywhere, let's begin to target your search. Some places and activities such as singles clubs and dating services are specifically designed for one reason: to bring single people together. However, they are not designed to help you meet a specific "type" of candidate. Nevertheless, some of these time-tested places might be useful, and we'll discuss those in the next chapter.

In this chapter you will investigate places that are not primarily designed for matchmaking such as health clubs, spas, country clubs, tennis/golf clubs, league sports, classes, volunteer organizations, vacations, etc. We will concentrate on targeting your search based on the activities that both you and your ideal candidate are interested in. Focusing on targeted activities will not only save you money, but also save you time, because you are participating in some of them already.

If fitness is important to you, and that is something that you would also like in a candidate, you have a better chance of meeting a fitness-minded person at a health club than at a singles club.

Targeted, non-singles oriented activities are good ways to meet like-minded people, but they are especially useful for people who are shy about events designed solely to find a mate. You can just relax and enjoy the event, without the pressure of partner-hunting! Most importantly, activities that suit your values, lifestyle and interests will tend to attract others with similar needs and tastes. If you love the outdoors, you'd enjoy that nature walk with your local hiking group – with or without a love search. Happily, it is also a great place for you to meet single candidates who fit your qualifications!

Summary

- ♥ Non-singles-specific places and activities are good locales for recruiting love because you can do the activities you already enjoy.

- ♥ You have a much better chance of meeting a specific type of person than if you merely go to a place where the only common denominator is that people are single!

Singles events definitely have the edge on quantity. Let's face it – not everyone in the health club is single. But just because there are tons of singles in one place doesn't guarantee that you will find even one person who suits your job description. Quantity doesn't necessarily bring quality.

> Diane said:
> Before I began using *Recruiting Love*, I spent a lot of time at big singles events, wishing and hoping. I thought this was a good opportunity – where there were many singles congregated together. One day, I read that the hottest new dance club in town was going to be open to 800 Jewish singles. I'm Jewish, but I don't actively practice, and I wanted to meet other non-religious Jews. This event seemed great, because I could meet lots of Jewish men at in one place at one time, and be one of the first in my crowd to go to this new dance club.
>
> Since this was such trendy place, I planned my outfit accordingly, wearing a very eye-catching, super-short, body-hugging dress. I'd been working out at the gym, and wanted to show off the results of all my hard work. As I waited in line at the check room with my raincoat, I realized that something was strange. Although this was a hot club, all the women around me seemed to be wearing very modest, conservative dresses, not of the sort that one usually sees at a trendy club. The majority of the men wore black suits and hats or yarmulkes! I realized that the event had been staged for ultra-religious, or Orthodox singles. Modest dress is an important part of their lifestyle.

> I immediately felt out of place in my revealing outfit! Furthermore, I wasn't interested in dating someone whose beliefs ran to Orthodoxy, and they wouldn't be interested in dating me. Since I was already there, I decided to stick around and enjoy the club, but I just couldn't. I covered myself up and stood at the edge of the dance floor, miserable, out of place, and sweating in my raincoat. I couldn't maintain a conversation with any of the men — they could see that I wasn't their best candidate. After about a half an hour I gave up and went home. I learned that just because there are a lot of singles in one place, it doesn't mean that they're going to be people I'd be interested in, or vice-versa.

Contrast Diane's story with Jim's. Jim frequently patronized trendy clubs, and met lots of interesting women. Occasionally, he even found someone that he dated more than once. But mostly, Jim bought women drinks and had a lot of "one night stands." Finally, he realized that although he met hundreds of women at clubs, he would be better off targeting his search to smaller, more select groups containing the types of women he wanted to meet. Jim was artistic and creative, and he wanted that quality in his candidate also. He enrolled in a watercolor painting class, and met more suitable women than he met in a year of waiting and hoping in the club scene.

What Type of Candidate Do You Really Like?

When you created the *You Company* candidate job description in Chapter 2, you determined the characteristics that your ideal candidate must have. This narrowed your parameters and focused your search. You might have determined that your ideal candidate has to be intelligent, caring and sensitive, even-tempered, have a good sense of humor, and be ready for marriage and family. Defining these *intrinsic* qualities was the first part of the research process. Now, in order to fine-tune and target your search, you have to define what "types" of individuals you are most attracted to.

The "Envisioning Exercise"

Put down this book for a moment, close your eyes, and visualize your ideal candidate.

- ♥ What vision immediately springs to mind?
- ♥ What images do you see?
- ♥ What setting is your ideal candidate in?
- ♥ What is s/he doing in that setting? What does s/he look like?

Now define that vision in words, like the following two examples:

► Sharon said:

Based on my job description, I knew I wanted a financially secure, intelligent, caring, and self-assured man who definitely didn't want a family. I initially envisioned my candidate as a businessman in a suit, but to my surprise, when I did the envisioning exercise I saw a man riding a brown and white horse, against a backdrop of tall mountains (probably out West), leading other men on horses in rounding up a herd of cattle, and wearing outdoor clothes! Upon reflection, I realized that besides the intrinsic characteristics I wanted, there were other factors involved that would make someone particularly attractive to me. True, my ideal candidate might be a financially successful businessman or a professional, but he'd be most attractive me if he also loved the outdoors, was a leader, and was adventurous and athletic.

► Mark said:

I knew the most important intrinsic qualities my candidate needed were: intelligence; healthy self-esteem, the ability to make me laugh, ready to marry and have a family; and a true romantic personality. I initially thought that I'd be most interested in someone who was in a "helper profession" like a nurse or an elementary school teacher. When I did the envisioning exercise however, my ideal candidate appeared as a college professor in a suit, explaining a complex formula on the blackboard to her students. To my surprise, I also clearly saw her wearing a campaign button on her jacket! As I thought about my vision, I realized

> that I'd be most attracted to a person who was a political activist and an intellectual! I began volunteering for a local politician—something I'd always wanted to do, anyway. When this politician participated in the college's "civic affairs" day, I volunteered to sit at the information table. It's probably no surprise that I met my ideal candidate (now my wife) that day. She was a biology professor who stopped by at the table!

The mental image you conjure up of your ideal candidate has far less to do with the rational analysis you did earlier, and much more to do with your emotional "gut feelings." The emotional and the rational are not mutually exclusive, however. When you combine your *intrinsic* requirements together with the *type* of person you'd ideally like to be with, you will have developed a *total* view of your ideal candidate!

Now, define your vision. Close your eyes again and envision your ideal candidate. What comes to mind? Fill in the following blanks:

When I close my eyes, my ideal candidate appears to be in (describe setting):

_____

_____

doing (describe action or activity):

_____

and wearing/looked (describe overall look or outfit):

_____

_____

_____

I also saw (describe any other important details):

_____

_____

_____

How to Target the Best Locales

You now have a clear and comprehensive picture of your ideal candidate. Now that you have this knowledge, it's obvious that you'll have the best odds in the places where that person is likely to be, in the highest numbers, and most often! In other words: *"If you want honey, you go where there's a hive!"* Keep in mind, however, that human beings are very complex and can't really be stereotyped or pigeonholed — there are infinite combinations of qualities.

Suppose that you are attracted to rich and famous-type people on the level of Malcolm Forbes. If your first inclination is to look for such a candidate in the playgrounds of the rich and famous, you'd be right — it's highly likely you'd find that type of candidate there. But Mr. Forbes was also an adventurous man who liked motorcycles and hot air balloons. He appreciated and collected priceless works of art from all over the world.

And he was an intellectual, who created and ran a highly esteemed business publication! You might find a Malcolm Forbes-type candidate in any one of these other locales as well.

Review your envisioning exercise statement. Decide what the **most dominant** theme of your vision is, and then choose one or two additional themes. Sharon, for example, realized that her ideal candidate definitely had to be an outdoors-type person, but he also needed to be adventurous and athletic. Mark felt that his ideal candidate had to be an intellectual and academic-type person first, and he was also seeking someone who liked to get involved in political causes.

To help you jump-start your thinking, here's a list of some popular characteristics of people. This isn't complete by any means, but it will get you started!

- Active/sports-oriented: S/he likes to participate and/or watch about any type of sport you can think of. This type of person may also be very interested in personal health and fitness.

- Activist/politically-minded: People most interested in community and current causes, and who usually try to influence public opinion and policy. This type of person may be in politics, work in a non-profit organization, and/or act as a volunteer.

- Adventurous: Daring and willing to take risks—that sums up the adventurous person. Adventurous types like excitement and danger both physical (e.g. hang-gliding, fire walking, stock car racing) and mental (gambling, high finance, body piercing).

- Creative/artistic: Creative types have a broad imagination as well as artistic or intellectual skills. They may work in a creative field (art, dance, writing, comedy, music, etc.). This type may just be someone who looks and acts in an unusual way.

- ♥ Highly educated/intellectual/academic: S/he must have a minimum of a college degree, and usually has one or more graduate degrees. This type is interested in lifelong learning, is a literary and cultural sophisticate, and is preoccupied with the world-at-large.

- ♥ Older singles: Obviously, "older" is a relative term, depending on your own age. We are defining this type as any man or woman who is over 65 years of age and is interested in a romantic relationship.

- ♥ Outdoor-lover: This type of person loves anything out-of-doors, from any outdoor sports to picnics, nature walks, garden groups, camping, fishing, hunting and environmental and wildlife conservation.

- ♥ Professional: S/he has met the high standards of a vocation or occupation requiring advanced education and training, and involving intellectual skills (e.g.. medicine, theology, law, engineering, and teaching).

- ♥ Single parent: Single parents are defined as any natural or adoptive parent who has total or part custody of one or more minor children.

- ♥ Special interest: This type of person has a distinctive, particular, or unique lifestyle, interest, need, or curiosity which is of paramount importance to him/her (e.g.. nudist, vegetarian, devout religious beliefs).

- ♥ Ultra-wealthy/celebrity: S/he must have either money or fame on a global scale (millions of dollars and/or instant public recognition). For our purposes, this person can also be a local celebrity, or one of the wealthiest people in a small town or city.

These types of people can be found everywhere you look, but there are specific places where you are **most likely** to find them. Where are the *best* places to find your ideal candidate? The following chart will give you some ideas of where you might begin to look, **but it is by no means inclusive**.

Let's say that you'd like to find someone adventurous, with some creative and intellectual characteristics too. Look at the chart on the following page to see where someone who matches this profile might be found. Then, select the activities which most closely match your own interests, geographic considerations, finances, and lifestyle. This should give you some good ideas, but don't forget to brainstorm on your own!

TYPE	WHERE TO FIND THEM	VACATION SUGGESTIONS[1]
Educated/ Intellectual/ Academic	Colleges, universities, professional societies and schools, college and alumni clubs, book circles, advanced degree/continuing education classes, museums, libraries, lectures, cultural events, MENSA	Educational travel, professional or university sponsored travel, conferences and seminars
Professional	Same as above, but target to specific profession. Check the library and the Internet local chapters of national and international professional associations	National and international association meetings and conferences
Adventurous	Doing dangerous, risky, exciting or unusual activities (skydiving, bungee jumping, fire walking, rodeo riding, mountain climbing), any type of racing event, body piercing parlors, after-hours clubs	Special interest vacations (race-car driving school, skiing), archeological digs, unusual vacation destinations

Outdoor Lover	Running, biking or sailing clubs, environmental groups, garden clubs, botanical gardens, nature trails, zoos	Eco-tours, dude ranches, camping, safaris
Active/ Sports-Oriented	Health clubs, company sports teams local sports leagues, dances and dance classes, sports classes	Special interest vacations (golf or tennis weekends), baseball, basketball, sailing camps for adults, sports halls of fame, spa vacations
Activist/ Political	Any type of volunteer organization, Government centers, marches and demonstrations, nonprofit organizations	Wherever you can help others (volunteering to help the victims of a disaster, Habitat for Humanity, etc.)
Creative/ Artistic	Community theater, choir, orchestra, dance groups, comedy groups, art galleries, open university classes, cultural events, craft fairs	Educational and cultural travel, museums, theater and concerts, galleries

TYPE	WHERE TO FIND THEM	VACATION SUGGESTIONS[1]
Single Parent	PTA meetings, picking up your child after day care or school, getting involved with extra-curricular activities, Parents Without Partners, zoos, children's stores	Child-oriented travel or family vacation destinations (Disneyland, theme parks) major tourist attractions, amusement parks, especially on weekends
Older Singles	Almost any local activities for older adults can be found in the local Yellow Pages, newspaper or over the Internet	Elderhostel, cruises, special travel catering to older adults
Wealthy Celebrity[2]	Yachting, horse racing and polo, financial and business clubs, gourmet societies and wine connoisseur clubs, charity events, exclusive hotels, spas, or country clubs	Fly first class, ultra-deluxe and trendy destinations, out of the way places, chartered yachts, deluxe spas, hotels and casinos

[1] To save money on these vacations, look for travel agencies that specialize in singles events.

[2] Keep in mind that this group of people often participates in activities that most of us cannot easily afford. If you're serious about recruiting from this group, you must be prepared to dress and act accordingly.

Recruiting Love is an Investment

We know some of the activities we've suggested take time and money, but you don't have to have a lot of either to recruit effectively. If your finances don't allow you to attend a luxurious golf camp, perhaps you can still attend the eight-week golf class offered by your local recreation association — with the same result! Volunteering for sports-related organizations costs nothing, and you might even be able to save some money, as some of the expenses are paid by the organizations. Just remember to have an open mind, and select activities that you will enjoy and will maximize your efforts.

How to Keep a Dating Log (& Why You Need To!)

While we were conducting our own love searches, we created a special recruitment tool — the *Dating Log*. We believe this will be one of your most important tools, and we urge you to use it before and during your recruitment phase, and throughout the candidate selection process.

For a business project, you would probably keep a record of the hours that you worked, the expenses you incurred, a list of people with whom you interacted and maybe even notes of what was said at project meetings. A dating log is similar, except in this case, you are charting not only your progress, but also specific information about your candidates and your feelings about them.

Your dating log will be your permanent record of your experiences, and it will prove invaluable in keeping you on track. It's a place to record your assessment of your dates, the types of people you are selecting, and the progress and success of your "recruiting program."

It will become a barometer for identifying your own patterns and behavior as you search for the candidate who will permanently fill your *You Company* position.

> Ian said:
> I wasn't sure how the dating log would work at first, but I decided that if I was going to take the time to recruit love, I should do it right. So I tracked every one of my dates from first contact right to the end. At first I used the prepared form, but I soon found that I actually enjoyed writing about my dates. The log helped me learn about myself and to identify my dating patterns — good and bad. When a date went well, I had a triumph to record for future reference. If it went badly, I knew that writing about it in my log would at least make a miserable date into a learning experience. Reporting about my candidates made me view dating more rationally — the way I view my professional work. This made the entire process seem less humiliating. I followed my plan and have been happily married to my ideal candidate for six years.

When you go through your dating log, you'll see what you're doing right, as well as what might be going wrong. After you've been recruiting candidates for a while, your dating log will show you patterns you might not otherwise recognize. It will show you whether you're really selecting and dating candidates that fit your job description, identify situations where your image or behavior could use adjustment, and confirm whether you're looking for candidates in the most appropriate places. The log will also help you remember information about your candidates for later reference.

With a dating log, no date is wasted because it's a learning experience for the next time. It provides a unique "history" of your love search that you'll refer to frequently. Make sure you're the only one who will read it, so it will be a safe place to record your feelings, assessments and comments. You can say anything you like, and not be judged for it.

Naturally, we hope you won't need it, but your dating log also serves as an invaluable review of your previous experiences to help you decide what direction you might take the next time around.

Creating and Maintaining Your Dating Log

The dating log will be priceless to you and it won't cost much more than a dollar to create. It's also very easy to do. Get any kind of notebook you like. (We suggest lined paper in a bound book where the pages won't fall out.) If you're high tech, you can set your log up on a computer, so long as no one else is likely to find your files. **Never** keep your log on the office computer—if you've worked in an office for any length of time, you know your files aren't private! You can also record your information on tape — but eventually you'll need to transcribe it to hard copy.

There's no specific formula for creating and maintaining your dating log, but for those who would rather use a set form, we've created a basic format. Feel free to add whatever you wish. Be consistent. Record **every** date, including contacts, experiences and reactions leading up to the date, and a "postmortem" afterwards. Don't wait too long to do your entry, even if it's only a small one. Here's the basic information you will want to record for each entry no matter what format you use:

- ♥ Entry date
- ♥ Date, time and place of the "interview"
- ♥ Candidate's full name (address/phone if you have it).
- ♥ Other pertinent information about the candidate (two kids from previous marriage, lived on a commune, loves caviar, red hair is natural, loved Howdy Doody as a child, etc.).
- ♥ Where you made the contact or how the date came about (introduced by a friend, stepped on your toe at the post office, is the tai chi instructor's brother, etc).
- ♥ Substance and result of the contact/date (what did you do, how did the date go, how did you leave things between you, does the date require a follow-up, etc.).

After entering this information, the rest of the log is up to you. Here's a sample entry to give you some ideas.

DATING LOG ENTRY for Susan Single

Entry Date: 6/1/95   **Date Was On:** 5/28/95

Entry For: John Solo

Home Address: 25 Main Street, Anytown, US 19344

Office Address: Don't have yet

Phone Number (H): 384-9953   **(W):** Don't have yet

Age: 43   **Height:** Approx 6'2"   **Weight:** average

Occupation: College Professor (Political Science)

How We Met: a Syracuse University mentoring function for new undergraduate students

Specific points/impressions I might need later: John was very outgoing and I was attracted to his bright eyes and approachable smile. He told me he's looking for a serious relationship but has never been married (he's 43, could signal a problem). He called the day after I gave him my card (over anxious or interested?). Has a passion for old movies, likes Marlon Brando and belongs to a movie-buff organization. Enjoys gourmet food (a plus). Wore a tweed jacket with patches on the elbows. Wore the same jacket and an ugly tie for our first date (no other clothes?) Aside from that, I don't see any major liabilities yet.

Other personal data I might need to know: (Note: you might not have much of this in your first entry on a candidate, but fill these points in as you get them later on: more on appearance, education, current/prior marital status, kids, salary, living arrangements, car, home (own or rent?), travel preferences, food preferences, major likes and dislikes, any mutual friends or colleagues, hobbies, pets, etc.)

Our first date was: Coffee and dessert at the Star coffee house at Main and 2nd Street-my choice.

Details of our date: John was on time and carried a paperback travel guide (Fodors?). He's going to a professional conference in Paris next week and will be out of town for two weeks. At the coffee bar (Star on Second) he suggested I hold a table for the two of us, and asked if it would be okay for him to pay for my coffee and cake (considerate). He only drinks black coffee and his "cake" was a sugar-free muffin (sort of strange). We talked about travel and a bit about a transfer student he's trying to motivate. He didn't say much about his family or his past relationships, but I don't get the feeling he's had a major relationship for some time. All in all, a pleasant but not spectacular first encounter. He's about to go away so I won't hear from him for a few weeks, but he said he'd call when he gets back — I'd certainly consider another date.

Specific high/low points: At one point John went to make a phone call and he was away for at least ten minutes. When he returned he wouldn't discuss the call, but he seemed sort of agitated. High point was that he said he'd send a postcard from Paris (probably means he wants to see me again otherwise he wouldn't bother).

How the date ended: John walked me to my car and waited until I was inside and mouthed "I'll call you" through the window.

Follow up plans: If I don't hear from him within three weeks, I'll probably give him a call.

Assessment based on candidate requirements: Based on minimal information, John appears to suit my major requirements. He's somewhat set in his ways and argued with me about something stupid (parking regulations) at one point. There's some chemistry—maybe he'll grow on me. I'd say he's still a candidate.

Strategies to follow/future plans: John appears to like "emancipated females" so calling him first won't bother him if I decide that I want to do this before he calls me after he returns from Paris — I'll see how I feel.

I would rate this date: (Note: use any categories you wish, and also use them for any follow-up dates/contacts).

	A definite winner!
√	A promising step in the right direction.
	Worth a second date.
	Not horrible, but once was enough.
	A dating disaster!

Remember, this log is for your use only. No one is going to grade you on it, your promotion doesn't depend on it, and there's no one "right way" to record the information. Write whatever you want, whenever you want, for as long as you want. You may find that notations become part of your daily routine. And, like any other regular activity, there may be times when you don't feel like doing it even if you know you should. Resist the urge to skip it, as a log with gaps won't be as useful as a complete one. Keep your dating log faithfully and accurately, and you'll enjoy the rewards!

=== **THE BOTTOM LINE** ===

"The primary questions for an adult are not why or how, but when and where." Eugen Rosenstock-Huessy

From the desk of: The Advice Sisters

TO: *You Company* Recruiter

FROM: Alison and Jessica

RE: Summary of Chapter 4: Targeting the *You Company* Candidate Search (Pinpointing Specific Locales)

1. Keep alert for networking and recruiting opportunities everywhere by keeping an open mind and by being approachable.

2. Some locales are best for targeting particular "types" of candidates.

3. To help pinpoint the specific locales where your ideal candidate might be, it's helpful to define the "type" of candidate you really like.

4. The dating log is an essential tool for the recruitment and selection process. It will provide a record of your search, help you remember specific candidate data, identify your dating patterns, and aid in selection.

5. Your dating log can be in any form you wish because it is for your eyes only. To be effective, data must be entered for each candidate both regularly and accurately.

Summary Blueprint

From the desk of: The Advice Sisters

Today's Date: _____

   1. Before you target specific locales, you need to define the type of candidate you want.

I will complete this by: _____

   2. Use the suggestions in this chapter to target specific activities and locales for your search.

I will complete this by: _____

   3. Schedule recruiting activities weekly in your calendar. If you want to try something new, get information (call, write, ask friends, etc.).

I will complete this by: _____

   4. Create your dating log, and begin recording information about each candidate and contact.

I will complete this by: _____

   5. Go on to read Chapter 5.

I will complete this by: _____

Action Memo

On this page, I can hit either single's groups or septic tanks.

From the desk of: The Advice Sisters

TO: *You Company* Recruiter

FROM: Alison and Jessica

RE: Chapter 5: Covering all the bases
(ideas and places to broaden your search)

In the last chapter you targeted specific places to recruit your chosen type of candidate. However, good candidates can sometimes be found in more general places. In this chapter, we'll suggest some of the most time-tested places and ways to broaden your search.

By now you've probably gotten the idea that there are endless opportunities to meet people almost everywhere. The whole point of *Recruiting Love* is to target your search and "type" of candidate so that you maximize your recruiting time. Along with the specific places suggested in Chapter 4, you should also consider some more general, less-targeted social activities.

We know that your time is precious and you may not have enough of it to do every activity we suggest, but if you add a few of these general methods to your plan, you'll be sure that you haven't missed out on any good candidates that might turn up in these "markets."

To help you schedule the activities that you'd enjoy most, we've provided "types" of dating styles to help you select some general ideas. Which one(s) fit you best?

- ♥ **If you like dressing for dates and being with a crowd:** singles bars, groups and clubs may be fun.

- ♥ **If you like quiet conversation with just a few people:** a progressive dinner, a dining club, a matchmaker or a dating service may be more your style.

- ♥ **If you're looking to meet people and try something new:** alternative university classes might be a fun way to do both.

- ♥ **If you'd rather write than talk:** the Internet or a personal ad could add a new dimension to your search.

- ♥ **If you like to make your own fun and prefer spontaneous, casual dates:** small theme dinners or dining clubs might be your style.

- ♥ **If you enjoy an element of risk:** any large gathering, advertising with friends for dining partners, or even a blind date could provide a challenge.

- ♥ **If you like the tried-and-true:** a dating service or a matchmaker could broaden your search.
- ♥ **If you're open-minded:** try everything we suggest in this chapter at least once!

Just Another Type of "Business Meeting"

If you saying: "I'm pretty busy — how am I going to fit all this into my schedule?" remember that recruiting love is a job — just one that you've assigned to yourself. Interviewing candidates is just a unique type of business meeting.

Often, business situations such as cocktail parties, the boss to dinner, etc. can make you want to flee the room, but you know that they can pay big dividends. The same can be said for recruiting activities which are difficult for you. If you remember that these are all just different types of business meetings you will get through them and reap the huge rewards. (And we promise, the rewards are better than any business meeting!)

It's important that you put candidate interviewing high on your list of priorities. It is also important that you **plan and schedule** it into your week. Since you are single, some people may assume that you have loads of free time. You may be asked to stay late at the office, even if it isn't an emergency. If you have already scheduled a love-recruiting activity on your calendar, don't automatically agree to cancel it. Tell the truth: you've got an important obligation that you must fulfill.

If you've read this far, you must realize that the more targeted your search, the more effective it will be. In the previous chapter, we described some of the targeted activities which will help you to conduct a good love search. However, we also said that good single candidates can be found virtually everywhere, and there are any number of traditional ways to meet them. As you'll see, some are more effective than others.

The Singles Bar Scene

You may have purchased *Recruiting Love* thinking that you could avoid singles bars altogether. We agree that you CAN and you SHOULD! The atmosphere in bars and clubs isn't conducive to finding love: they're usually poorly lit, hot, crowded, often smoky, and so noisy that you can't hold anything more than a very superficial conversation. And, if you drink, you may discover that the person who looked so great at night doesn't look so wonderful in the daylight!

We can't deny that matches have been made in such places, but bars and clubs are very "hit or miss," and you're tired of wishing and hoping! We think your chances of finding your ideal candidate in a bar or club are very poor, but they're fine for occasional fun, especially if you enjoy dancing, drinking, dressing up, and lots of noise in a high-energy atmosphere.

Singles Clubs and Groups

The famous bank robber, Willies Cyton, said that he robbed banks because: "That's where the money is!" Singles clubs, organizations and activities are teeming with singles; in fact you can't even belong to them unless you're unattached. Many of these groups are already targeted by special interest (religion, lifestyle, hobbies, etc.) so you can look at your *You Company* job description and closely target your selection. Singles groups offer activities to suit every interest and budget, and most are relatively low-cost. Many even offer travel opportunities and "matchmaker" services for members. Unfortunately, the pool of possibilities may be limited (depending on the size or type of group) and since it's an easy way to be around other singles, some of the participants may be "coasting," instead of actively recruiting.

> Ellen said:
> I belonged to a singles group for three years, and I participated in lots of activities. I figured that everyone there would be genuinely interested in meeting his or her match, but some people seemed more interested in just looking at people and finding fault with them, instead of finding a mate. After a while, I began to see the same faces over and over again and I realized I had to branch out if I was ever going to find someone special.

Don't put all of your energy into singles clubs. Although we have heard some happy stories, we've also heard them described as, "a last resort for the desperate," among other less-than-flattering terms. As we've said before, **targeted** activities should always be your primary objective, but a few general singles activities added to your plan will bring variety, and optimum "target range" to your search.

What's New? "Eating & Meeting" Activities

Imagine people sitting around a table talking, eating, and laughing. At first glance it looks like a holiday dinner with friends, but it's not — it's a singles "eating and meeting event!"

Eating and meeting is based on a simple concept. Everyone is busy, but everyone needs to eat sometime. (Besides, most people enjoy it!) As one attorney told us, "I've got to eat dinner anyway; why do it alone?"

There are many variations on the "eat and meet" theme, and many singles groups focus on gourmet dining and wine-tasting. Here are a few other types of "eating and meeting" activities to consider:

Bring-a-Friend Dinners

Our Dad always told us, "Nice people have nice friends!" We think so too, and particularly like this idea based on an old-fashioned "swap meet!"

Invite some single friends to dinner, and ask each to bring an unattached friend of the opposite sex. This lets everyone meet and mingle in a social setting where no one is a total stranger. Everyone knows at least one person in the room! There's no pressure to pair off, but if it happens, that's fine. The dinner doesn't have to be fancy; you're there for meeting more than eating. You can also make it a potluck (everyone brings a friend and a dish), a simple cocktail party, or even a dessert party.

Potluck Dinners and Theme Parties

Potluck parties are especially fun if there is a theme: beach party in winter, my favorite recipe, Halloween treats, etc. Ask each guest to specify whether s/he'll bring appetizers, salad, main dish, dessert or beverages.

Theme parties are great icebreakers, because they give everyone something to focus on besides meeting and eating. A favorite theme party centers around the

Superbowl, where everyone "eats and meets," but also watches the big game. Another centers around the Kentucky Derby. At this party, guests receive a badge bearing the name of one of the horses running in the Derby. Fried chicken, mint juleps, and other southern fare is served, and the guests gather around the TV to watch the race. Even the shyest party-goer can't help shouting and clapping for "his/her horse" to win! The guest with the winning badge gets a prize, but everyone has a chance to be a "winner," because the horse race always encourages the guests to relax, mix and mingle!

Progressive Dinner

The progressive dinner is lots of fun — just like an adult game of musical chairs — except no one is left without a place to sit! There are two basic varieties. In the first version a group of single people meet for a five course dinner, but they have cocktails in the first restaurant and then "progress" from restaurant to restaurant for appetizers, salad, entrees, and finally, to the last location for dessert. Each time the group moves, participants sit with someone else.

The second version is less dizzying, but still lets everyone meet many people during the course of just one dinner. The participants eat the entire dinner in one restaurant. Each member of the group gets a number when they sit down and after each course, people with odd numbers move one space around the table clockwise, and those with even numbers move one space counter-clockwise!

You'll probably find advertisements for progressive dinners at local singles clubs, in the newspaper, or in alternative university catalogues. Sometimes restaurants sponsor progressive dinners themselves. As you can imagine, it takes good organizational skills to arrange a progressive dinner, but many restaurants will be happy to cooperate with you in the planning. If you're going to plan one yourself, work out the details ahead of time with the restaurant(s); don't just show up on the spur of the moment. It also helps if you know your costs ahead of time and ask each person for payment in advance — you'll avoid the awkward moment when the check comes! If you're going to do a progressive dinner with courses at different restaurants, select places within walking distance of each other — otherwise you'll end up with stragglers course after course!

You can also plan the "home version" of the progressive dinner with several friends who live nearby. Make creative invitations, and provide the name of the host/hostess for each course, along with directions.

Dining Clubs

We know of one informal dining club in New York City that has been meeting in the same Chinese restaurant every Tuesday evening for years. The original group has expanded to include their children, their children's friends, selected relatives, and anyone else wants to come to dinner with a regular member. This group is an eclectic mix of young and old, singles and couples, regulars and guests. However, some dining clubs consist of a just core group of singles who meet on a regular basis for breakfast, lunch or dinner in the same or different restaurants, or in each others' homes. Each participant is encouraged to bring new friends, and each person pays his or her own bill. No matter how you set up your dining club, it's a fun and relaxed way to share a meal with folks you know, all while meeting new people.

Wanted: Dining Partners!

You may be saying, "But my group of single friends is too small!" Why not advertise for more participants? We've seen this done quite a bit in recent years with great success. A group of friends pools their resources and places a personal ad calling for a set number of respondents to join the group for an elegant dinner. The friends each give a short description of themselves and what they're looking for, just as in a regular personal ad. When the responses roll in (what fun!), the friends select the best of the bunch and invite them to dinner at a local restaurant. It's a unique way to share expenses, excitement and participation with your friends, and create a pool of "guests" far greater than if you'd just chosen them one at a time. However, you still get some of the benefit of targeted recruiting, because at least some of the candidates meet your requirements!

I Thought I'd Finally Finished With School!

Remember how easy it was to meet people when you were still in school? You're all in class for a common purpose, so there's always something to talk about! If you're not interested in a degree, consider the infinite adult learning classes ranging from gourmet cooking to ballroom dancing. You can find them in the Yellow Pages under Adult Education, with titles such as: *First Class, Open University, Adult Learning Center,* etc. These classes are fun. You can try something new, and get the added bonus of seeing potential candidates as well. Many classes even emphasize group exercises, which make for great possibilities!

> Samantha said:
> I'm basically shy, and thought that a class would be an ideal way for me to get to know someone in a more natural setting. There were so many interesting classes that I didn't know which to choose, so I called the school and asked, "Which classes are likely to have a lot of single guys?"
> I was directed to *Improving Personal Communication*, which was certainly something I could benefit from, anyway. When I looked around the room, I saw three men that looked particularly interesting. One of them immediately sat down and paired up with someone else. The second man and I did a communication exercise in class (no chemistry there) but the third guy intercepted me at the door after class. He told me that he wouldn't usually be so forward, but now that he'd spent an entire evening trying to boost his communication skills, would I be willing to have a cup of coffee with him? That's how I met Andrew, my true love match, that night!

Most adult learning classes aren't restricted to singles, but some classes attract singles in high numbers. Obviously, *Living Single in the City* is a safer bet than *Remodel Your Kitchen*.

Most of these classes are very affordable, but if your budget doesn't allow for tuition, offer to help out at the school. Many will then let you take classes at no cost.

Before you dismiss this idea, think again. Many classes attract lively, interesting, and educated people who share similar interests. Why not try a one-night class? By the way, one of us met her husband that way!

Love in the Workplace

The workplace is not a place to concentrate your love search; however, sometimes relationships do spring up among business contacts and coworkers. Be very careful! Some do have happy endings, but that's more the exception. If you get involved with someone at work, you may face serious consequences. If the relationship doesn't work out, you may be uncomfortably and constantly reminded of it. At worst, an office affair could cause either or both of you to lose your jobs or damage your careers.

The Internet: Looking for Love In Cyberspace

If you have a computer at home and subscribe to an on-line service, there are lots of opportunities to meet people in cyberspace. We've heard both pros and cons. The downside is that, like a personal ad, you can't see who you're communicating with and only know what they tell you. Also, just like the personal ad, you're dealing with a stranger, and you need to be careful when giving out personal information or agreeing to meet face to face. On the plus side, the Internet opens up a whole new world of possibilities to meet people you'd never find otherwise. Furthermore, you can use the Internet to get information on singles clubs, groups, concerns, activities etc. There are even "chat" groups where you can talk with lots of like-minded singles all at once!

For more information, read Lorilyn Bailey's *The Complete Book of Online Romance*. See page 240.

The "Personals"

Personal ads gained popularity in the 70s, but some resisted the practice on the grounds that "no one nice" would place or answer ad for love. By the 90s, the stigma of personal ads has all but evaporated. We believe that placing or answering a personal ad is a viable way to meet people, as long as you employ honesty, caution, and common sense.

Writing and answering personal ads is a genuine skill, and we could write an entire book on it. In *Recruiting Love*, however, it's just one more method to broaden your love search. Personal ads can be fun, but you also need savvy to play the personals safely and successfully. Therefore, we'll devote more time to them than the other strategies.

When an employer decides to hire someone, s/he usually writes a job description and places a help-wanted ad based on the job requirements. If the ad clearly describes the position and it is placed in appropriate publications, the employer can expect many good responses from qualified candidates. Personal ads work the same way — they're help-wanted ads for love!

Personal ads let you advertise for candidates who meet your specifications. Once you place the ad, you can sit back and receive letters from qualified people describing how they want to satisfy your needs (and theirs!) If you'd rather respond to an ad, you can "shop" the personals (just like you'd peruse the help-wanted ads) until you find "job descriptions" and "company profiles" that interest you. Once you send a letter, you wait to be called for an "interview." Your *You Company Job Description, You Company Profile*, and envisioning exercise from Chapter 4 will help you.

Covering All The Bases   107

I'm six foot four, 210 pounds, and very, very gentle.

If you're lucky, you'll get the perfect candidate. You also might not get anyone who fits your job description, or someone who thinks s/he is perfect, but really isn't. The more skillful you are at playing the personals, the better your results will be.

> David said:
> I've been thinking of responding to some personal ads, or maybe even writing one of my own, but I've been intimidated because I'm not a strong writer and all of the ads seem so clever — I don't think I could find anything that witty to say.

Clever ads do attract attention, but you don't have to be a writer on the scale of Hemingway or Dickens to be successful. The secret is to **clearly** and **honestly** describe yourself and your ideal candidate in as few words as possible. (Most places charge by the word.) Answering ads costs little or nothing, but you have to wait for someone to choose you and you don't get to pick from that enticing selection of letters!

Just like on the Internet, there's always the potential for misrepresentation in a personal ad. Most people we spoke to told us that, chemistry aside, the people they met were "pretty much" as they represented themselves. We didn't hear many stories about people who blatantly lied about themselves, and we weren't told terrible tales about undesirables using ads for nefarious purposes! In fact, most of the people who write and respond to ads are normal, productive citizens!

> Annette said:
> I began answering personal ads on a dare from a friend. The first one was from Dan, a businessman who told me that he placed the ad because he was too busy for lots of social activities. I fit his requirements: average height and build, blue eyes, well educated, and interested in exotic travel, dining, and walks on the beach.
> I was nervous about meeting someone through the personals, but Dan was just what he said he was: good looking, intelligent, and easy to get along with. Unfortunately, we both could tell that there was no chemistry, but Dan treated me to a wonderful dinner and we both had a nice time.
> After that, I went out with lots of people through personal ads. None of the people turned out to be "toads." In fact, I met some candidates (politician, record producer, opera singer, calligrapher) that I would have never met otherwise.

Annette is now happily married, and, you guessed it, she met her husband through the personals!

How Do I Know What to Say?

Before you begin, refer to your candidate assessments from Chapter 2, and make sure to accurately reflect the *You Company's* candidate job description. If you're answering an ad, be sure you meet the basic requirements described in the ad, and make sure the person who placed the ad meets your basic requirements. Even though you're responding to the ad, you're still the *You Company* recruiter!

Whether you're placing or answering an ad, you'll want to provide some basic information about yourself (age, sex, appearance, education, occupation in general terms, etc.).

If you're placing an ad, you'll have to carefully select your most important requirements. Ad space is expensive. If you want a family, say so — you shouldn't waste your time with someone who definitely doesn't want children! And don't forget to mention anything that may be significant to your candidates. You might be perfectly willing to accept three Irish Setters into your home, but the people reading your ad might not.

To complete the picture, mention your hobbies, your idea of a romantic evening, your ultimate relationship goal — even the reason you answered or placed an ad in the first place.

Honesty is the Best Policy

In the working world, if you apply for a job and falsify your credentials, you'll be disqualified from the search, or worse, once you're found out, you'll be fired! You'll face similar consequences if you aren't honest with your personal ads or responses.

> Lorrie said:
> I answered Mike's personal ad, which said he was a 35-year old, successful advertising executive — trim, handsome, into tennis, and looking for marriage. We talked on the phone a few times, and he seemed perfect!
> On the night of our date, I arrived at the restaurant early. Soon afterwards, a huge, sloppy man came barreling into the restaurant and made

> a beeline for me. He wiped his sweaty face with one hand and extended the other. "Hey, I'm Mike," he wheezed. "I'm lucky I made it because I had to wait at Unemployment."
>
> I was struck dumb. Mike was nothing like he'd said in his ad and over the phone. I discovered that he was actually 55, and an out-of-work ad space salesman. It was true that he was looking for love, but he'd been married three times and was still in the process of separating from his last wife. He didn't play tennis. We actually had nothing in common.
>
> It's incredible, but Mike kept demanding to know why I wouldn't agree to a second date. "We have nothing in common — why didn't you just tell the truth?" I asked. "Sure I stretched the facts a bit," Mike admitted, "but I figured that no one would go out with me if I wrote: 'no looks, no job, no personality — please call.' This way I get quality babes and see, it worked!"

Mike wasted everyone's time, and his grandiose lying left his dates feeling disgusted and used. While there's no need to mention those extra five pounds, you should never completely fabricate who you are. You'll waste both your time, and the time of others.

This brings us to the question of photographs. If you ask for them, you are making a statement that appearance very important to you. Most people don't have a lot of recent photos sitting around to enclose with letters. Besides, just like a job reference, who would ever provide a bad one? And, we've heard some really bizarre stories of people who sent very old photos, and even photos of other people!

Precautions to Consider

As with any first encounter, don't identify yourself too specifically in a personal ad. Most people sign off with a first name or a unique, eye-catching moniker. (Remember *Sleepless in Seattle?*) *Cat-Woman, Skiing Fool, Happy Camper,* or *Musical Monica of Manhattan* will make your ad distinctive and memorable. When you place your ad, you will be assigned a mailbox or a voice mail number, so you should never have to reveal your address.

Is There a Shortcut For Writing the Responses?

NO! You'd never send a job resume without a cover letter, and you'd never send a cover letter that was obviously just a form letter. There is nothing quite so insulting as opening a letter which says: "Dear Personal Ad Writer." Your response has to be personal, but not elaborate — a brief note will suffice. It may be tempting, but resist the urge to be too creative in order to stand out. Writing a message on a container of take-out food and having it delivered, or writing a message on your jockey shorts, is best left for later!

Where do I Find These Personal Ads?

Many local magazines and newspapers have an entire classified section just for personal ads. Unless you're planning or willing to make a big move, you're best off with these local publications. You can also target your personal ad search through special interest publications and singles clubs. A little research will net many places to advertise.

Reading Between the Lines

As we stated earlier, treat personal ads just like a help-wanted ad. That means you have to be discriminating about which ads you answer. You wouldn't answer an ad for a computer programmer if you didn't know the first thing about computers. Personal ads work the same way. Your assets are not relevant if they're not what that employer wants or needs. Read between the lines of the personal ads and responses, and you'll see tip-off statements about the author's expectations:

- ♥ "for discrete liaison" (probably married)
- ♥ "seeking friendship" (probably that's it)
- ♥ "fun and hot times" (sex)
- ♥ "no smokers" (if they're specific, they mean it)
- ♥ "for whatever happens" (not sure what they want)
- ♥ "to meet my son" (Mom is placing the ad, beware — you're responding to the mother!)
- ♥ "for committed relationship" (not necessarily marriage),

In addition, the may contain abbreviations to help both the writer and reader save money and embarrassment. Some of the most popular are:

S=single	W=White	B=Black
H=Hispanic	A=Asian	F=female
M=male	BI- bisexual	J=Jewish
M=married	D=divorced	NS=non-smoking
G= gay	L= lesbian	PROF=professional

C=Christian/Catholic SWING= multiple sex partners
TV= transvestite TX= transsexual

Take these categories seriously. As we've said before, it's essential to know what you want, so you can effectively recruit that person.

Placing or Answering Ads by Voice Mail

Voice mail ads follow the same rules as regular personal ads. If you hate to write letters but are great on the telephone, voice mailboxes may be right for you. You'll still want to plan in advance what you're going to say, to alleviate nerves and to be sure you don't leave out anything important!

I've Written/Responded to an Ad — What's Next?

Once you've submitted your ad, don't forget to ask when it will appear, and when you could expect responses. Get a copy of the publication as soon as it comes out to make sure that your ad is actually there and that it's accurate. Then, enjoy those responses!

> Jane said:
> I was looking for a new way to put zip into my in my social life. Personal ads appealed to me because they incorporated adventure with writing — two things I really like. In all of my dating experiences, nothing was quite as exciting as coming home from a hard day and finding that big fat envelope of responses. I'd pour myself a glass of wine, and thoroughly enjoy reading those letters from all the men who wanted to meet me!

Reading all those response letters is fun, but it's still serious work for you — the *You Company* recruiter. Read the letters carefully, and select the ones you want to investigate further. Put comments in the margins so you don't have to re-read them. Then, rate the responses in order of preference, and use your dating log to list names and phone numbers (and any pertinent information that might come in handy later).

It's flattering to think that those who wrote to you didn't write to anyone else, but that's not usually the case. The sooner you call your top respondents, the more likely you'll schedule interviews with them before they become too booked up. Just like in job hunting, the early bird catches the worm.

If you're responding to an ad, do it as soon as possible. In business, employers often get inundated with resumes and only respond to the first group. Once you've written a response, keep in mind that just like answering a job classified ad, you may get an immediate response, or none at all.

Here are some tips to remember for a first contact:

- ♥ If you call when you have to catch the bus in a few minutes, you can't be relaxed. Call when you're alone and can talk. Evenings are usually best. Ask if this is a good time to talk. Remember, you are deciding whether you want to meet this person (and they, you).

- ♥ Have the respondent's letter and your dating log nearby to refer to while you talk.

- ♥ Identify yourself only as "the dog-lover who placed the ad in the Village Weekly." If the conversation is going well, reveal your first name only.

♥ If you get nervous on the telephone, write out a brief phone script. Agree whether or not you're going to speak on the phone again, or where you're going to meet. Exchange phone numbers, but don't exchange addresses. (You'll read more on how to handle personal information in Chapter 7.)

I've Made the Call: Now What Do I Do?

After you hang up, assess your notes (See, the dating log has already paid off!) and prepare for your date. One recruiter we know always asks women what their favorite flower is — and then shows up on the date with at least one in hand.

A first meeting should be short, public, and inexpensive. Although the ultimate goal may be to find a lifelong partner, you don't need to reveal too much at the first meeting.

> ▶ Don't be as blunt as Gus!
> I'll pick you up Sunday at noon so Bobby, my two-year-old can see if he likes you. If he approves, then we can go to the kiddie park for the afternoon — Bobby likes it there a lot.

By the way, an initial encounter isn't the appropriate time for your kids to meet your dates. Furthermore, we hope your idea of placing the personal ads was to meet a mate, not to hire a nanny.

If you find it is clearly not a match, don't draw it out. As harsh as it may seem, personal ads are a numbers game. You're the recruiter, and you've got to make tough decisions. If a candidate doesn't work out, you simply move onto the next one in a seemingly neverending supply of new possibilities. Here's what you could say if you're nervous about rejecting someone:

- ♥ "I think we're probably looking for different things."
- ♥ "I enjoyed meeting you but we really don't have as much in common as I'd hoped."
- ♥ "I don't want to have children and I can see that you're dying to be a father. I'm sure you'll find someone who wants the same thing you do."

We hope that you now feel confident enough to write or respond to a personal ad. If you're adventurous and open-minded and don't like to meet people in groups, personal ads may be just the thing for you!

For more information on personal ads, read Richard Coté's *Love By Mail*. See the Appendix.

Making Matches for Money: Matchmakers and Dating Services

There are many ways to meet someone, and we've described just a few. However, no discussion about meeting singles would be complete without some words about matchmakers and dating services. If you have a negative reaction any of these, please remember that you should consider many different options — and these people have been making successful love connections for a long, long time! They might possibly come up with your perfect candidate, although it depends greatly on the quality of the service, the type of search, and your requirements.

Some matchmaking services are more like personnel agencies (matching bodies to jobs) than executive recruiters (extensively searching for one perfect candidate) but if you're super-busy, picky or lazy, matchmakers might be a great option for you.

Do matchmakers and dating services really work? It depends. The downside is that they are profit-making **businesses** and, of course, they can only match you up with others who have signed up. Matchmakers and dating services make it easy to find candidates, so on one level, they're a decent option. However, we believe in the expression: "if you really want a job done right, do it yourself." Don't expect someone else to do your entire job for you or you'll miss too many good opportunities.

Before you sign up with a dating service, check it out carefully. Who has used them before? Were they successful? Why or why not? Were there problems with service once they signed up? What is the membership policy (a month, six months, a year, until you find someone?) How many contacts will you will be allowed to make, and can you refuse a date without it being "counted?" Can you get a refund? Ask for references and proof of their success rate, and if you're unsure, call the Better Business Bureau and see if anyone has lodged a complaint. Don't be pressured into making your listing too broad in order to get more matches.

If you use a matchmaker or dating service, your success will depend largely on the skill of the matchmaker, and how honestly and specifically you describe yourself and your needs. If cigarette smoke makes you gag, don't say you'll accept a smoker. If you hate sports, don't say you're a sports lover to impress men. If you do, you'll only suffer through date after date at soccer, hockey, basketball and football games!

ABC Dating Service #400003
Strong man with great hair and big chest seeking perfect match. Musically inclined, passion for drumming.

Like personnel agencies, dating services often match people using a computer database program. Some services also employ video dating, where you are filmed in a short videotape for prospective dates to view. This is great if you come across well on film and are extremely articulate and personable. It doesn't work well for people who are shy, don't speak well, or get nervous in front of a camera. In video dating, people tend to select those who look the best on tape, rather than those who might actually be best.

It's tempting to resort to matchmaking services because they hold out the promise of recruiting love without a lot of hassle, but it can cost a bundle, provide limited results, and waste a great deal of your precious recruiting time. If you go this route, make sure it's only one of many options you choose.

Making Matches for Free – The Fix-Up

We've left the fix-up, otherwise known as the "blind date," for last. Why? Because everyone knows that more toads have been kissed on blind dates than in any other dating arena. To be fair, however, a lot of happy couples have met through friends or relatives. We're not suggesting that you go out of your way to get fixed up, but remember that the fixer-upper genuinely cares for you, and sincerely wants to help. Thus, your chance of winding up on a date with someone dangerous is quite small.

The best advice we can give you about blind dates is: Don't turn one down without due consideration. Blind dates aren't 100% chance meetings, so you have some possibility of being compatible with your date. Ask your matchmaker about the candidate. If there's little chance the person can fit your job description, refuse the date.

However, if the person seems to have some potential, go for it! If you hate the idea of a blind date, ask the matchmaker to invite both of you to dinner or to a movie. That way, you have your mutual friend to turn to if things go sour! It might turn out to be a flop, but you just might "live happily ever after!"

> Ann said:
> I never thought much of blind dates, and suffered through my share of mismatches. Finally, I began recruiting love in earnest. I started volunteering, and at a fundraising event, I bumped into Wendy, an old college friend whom I hadn't seen for twenty years. Over dinner, I told her about my ideal candidate, and she insisted that she knew the perfect man for me! Jess was Wendy's neighbor and she swore he had practically every quality I wanted! The following week, I reluctantly went to her place for what I knew would be an endless evening with another disappointing man. I was shocked when the door opened and there was Jess — my soul mate! Jess must have felt the instant attraction too, because he came right over to me, held both my hands in his, and wordlessly gazed into my eyes — just like a scene from a romance novel. The better I got to know him, the more I realized that Jess had all of the qualities I wanted. We're planning our future together. After all my dating experiences, the last place I ever expected to meet my match was on a fix-up!

THE BOTTOM LINE

"A wise man will make more opportunities than he finds."
Sir Francis Bacon

From the desk of: The Advice Sisters

TO: *You Company* Recruiter

FROM: Alison and Jessica

RE: Summary of Chapter 5: Covering all the bases (ideas and places to broaden your search)

1. Good candidates can be found in more general markets, and you should investigate and incorporate some into your recruiting plan.

2. Your dating "style" will determine which recruitment activities will appeal to you most.

3. Don't forget! Recruitment activities are a priority, just like a business meeting or a family obligation. Don't cancel them unless you have a serious emergency!

Summary Blueprint

From the desk of: The Advice Sisters

Today's Date: _____

1. Investigate and select some general activities/locales to broaden the *You Company* candidate search.

I will complete this by: _____

2. Schedule some general recruitment activities each week in your planner or calendar. If you'd like to try a new activity, get information (call, write, ask friends, etc.).

I will complete this by: _____

3. Remember to record activity and dating information in your dating log.

I will complete this by: _____

4. Go on to Chapter 6.

I will complete this by: _____

Action Memo

124   Recruiting Love

From the desk of: The Advice Sisters

TO: *You Company* Recruiter

FROM: Alison and Jessica

RE: Chapter 6: Tools to Facilitate the Search

    This chapter gives you some of the essential tools & tips that are helpful in a love recruiter's search. You may know or have some of them already, but even the simplest of our suggestions can make your love search easier, safer, and more successful. Most of our suggestions cost little or no money.

15-Second Memo

Doctors carry their tools in black leather bags; fashion models use large totes. Every profession has tools of the trade, and love recruiters do too!

Obviously, tools for recruiting love are a little different from stethoscopes and pills for doctors, or lipstick and mascara for fashion models, but they're no less essential. You will use some of your dating tools at home, some you will carry with you when you go out; others, you won't even see — but all of them will be important to you.

The Answering Machine: a Recruiter's Best Friend

Diamonds are a girl's best friend and a dog is a man's best friend — but a love recruiter's best friend is an answering machine! **It is the number one essential tool for recruiting love.**

If you're one of the few who still balks at the idea of getting an answering machine or refuses to leave a message on anyone else's, consider the facts.

You are now a love recruiter. That means you'll be spending a lot of time on the phone "interviewing" prospective candidates. It's unprofessional to conduct a social life from work, not to mention you probably won't get any work done! Even if you are an executive with a secretary who is the model of discretion, it's not a good idea to have long or intimate personal conversations in your office. Unless you work alone in a completely closed work space (and few people do) there's at least one "snoop" in every office who will listen in on your conversations and share them with everyone.

> Rhonda said:
> I spend so much time at work that I figured my office would be the best place to get my personal calls. I confided in my secretary that I'd actively started dating and that I might soon be receiving a lot of personal calls from different men. I asked her to keep those messages out of the office's regular message box and hand them to me directly. After a week, I noticed that the conversation stopped every time I walked into a meeting. My secretary had been keeping my personal messages on her desk and someone had read them. Outrageous rumors quickly spread around the office — even to my boss!

If you've completed Chapters 2 through 5, you're probably recruiting candidates. We assume that you'll be at work all day and recruiting in the evening, so how will you know if you've gotten important calls?

Don't count on your roommate or family members to take your calls. They don't work for you and can't be expected to record all messages completely. Besides, this is private stuff! Your roommate, mother, little sister, etc. may tell your prospective dates that you snore, you were in the marching band in college, or you're out on a date with someone else. If you live with other people and share a phone line, consider putting in your own private line so your calls will go directly to your answering machine when you're not home.

An answering machine is loyal; it only says what you tell it to say. It's reliable; it accurately answers your messages 24-hours-a-day without complaining or quitting. It's never jealous; it won't two-time or sabotage you. It works in your best interests; it keeps unwanted callers away until **you** want to talk; and it is inexpensive; it costs less than a good dinner.

If you "just don't like machines," other options are voice-mail, and personal message services. Voice-mail works just like an answering machine, but you don't have any equipment in your home. You can get voice-mail through private service companies or your phone company, for a monthly charge. You can also get a personal answering service, but these are often staffed by exhausted moonlighters who frequently make mistakes.

Personalizing Your Greeting

Personalizing your answering machine greeting conveys a bit of your personality to everyone who hears it. A few bars of your favorite music is a good choice, but just make sure your greeting is short and tasteful. Howie wanted to express his love of sailing on his tape — but after two long verses of "Blow The Man Down," his callers were ready to jump overboard — without leaving a message! Mary unfortunately forgot about her business associates (and her mother!) who called her at home:

> Mary said:
> I thought it would be fun to leave a sexy greeting, and I got several positive comments from men about it. About a week later, I began getting an unusual number of hang-ups. I didn't make the connection between the hang-ups and my taped message until my mother called me, quite shocked! In my zeal to make my message "unforgettable," I forgot that business associates, friends and family also called me at home! A co-worker had called

Tools to Facilitate the Search 129

On top of SPAGHETTI
All covered with CHEESE
I lost my poor MEATBALL
When somebody SNEEZED

It rolled off the TABLE
And onto the FLOOR . . .

> my home, heard the sexy tape, and quickly spread the word. All the men in my office started called to listen to the message and then hung up! I'm still trying to live that one down!

It goes without saying that for safety reasons, your message should never state your last name, your address, or broadcast that you're on vacation. You can leave your beeper number for emergencies if you want callers to find you that way.

Often, a candidate's first impression of you will be over the phone, so remember your phone etiquette! When you leave a message, don't make it so long that no one else has room on the tape. Just leave your name, phone number, the date and time of your call, and a concise message.

An answering machine also serves another very important purpose: it allows you to screen your calls! Hopefully you won't need this feature too often, but it's good to know that it's there if you need it.

> ▶ Barbara said:
> It became clear to me that Chuck wanted an exclusive relationship when I didn't. I guess he didn't really get the message, because the next evening he called while my friend Bob was over. I told Chuck it wasn't a convenient time to talk. Then he demanded to know "who was there with me." I told him again that I couldn't talk but that I would call him back later, and then I hung up.
> For the next hour the phone rang constantly, upsetting me and irritating Bob. Finally, when Chuck

> called for about the twelfth time, Bob picked up the phone and shouted into the receiver: "Hey buddy, don't you get it? Barbara doesn't want to talk to you!" Chuck stopped calling, but if I had been screening my calls, none of this would have happened.

Manners Aren't Just for Amy Vanderbilt

Etiquette is not just for little old ladies who wonder whether or not to eat olives with a knife and fork. You'll want your love candidates to display good manners—so you must too. If it's been years since you've thought about "good behavior," we strongly suggest that you get an etiquette book. *Miss Manners* is particularly up-to-date and amusing, but *Emily Post* and *Amy Vanderbilt* are reliable, too. Your etiquette book can help you survive all sorts of sticky situations, and you'll be surprised how frequently you check it for advice. Start with the section on phone manners, and you'll quickly see how practical the rules are.

Be Impressive

As a love recruiter, you probably won't by driving up in a hot car, flashing your cash or wearing expensive clothes. Being truly impressive doesn't cost anything, and it's as basic as can be. **Be considerate, be amiable, be open minded, be a good listener, be a good sport, be fun to be with, and be genuinely interested in who you're with.**

Tools That Can (Literally) Save Your Life

The working world is set up not only to ensure the efficiency of its employees, but also to ensure their safety. Secretaries screen calls, security guards screen visitors, and employees use various types of tools and equipment to ensure that they are not injured. In dating, similar types of tools will help to ensure your safety, and increase your efficiency. Let's start with the most popular of all business tools — the business card.

Here's My Card

Every business person knows the value of a business card. It's how you establish your credentials, document your affiliation, and show where you can be contacted. We suggest a similar card, called a **personal card**, for recruiting love. It allows you to introduce yourself gracefully, rather than awkwardly scrounging for a pen and scribbling your number on a scrap of paper or a matchbook. (And, you can never be sure where that matchbook is going to end up!)

The personal card originates from the "calling card." These cards, which had only your name, were once used (and still are, in some circles) to leave brief messages, for enclosure with flowers and gifts, and to announce visitors. Your personal card will have your name **and** phone number and perhaps your beeper number, fax number, or e-mail address. Personal cards should be the same size as a business card, but you can be more creative with the color, card stock, and design. Be reasonable, though. Teddy bears belong on your pillow, not on your personal card. There is plenty of time for candidates to discover that your hobby is collecting insects — without pictures of beetles crawling across your card!

The Dating Kit

Once you have them, you will carry your personal cards with you wherever you go. In addition, there are other small, but essential, tools that can stop a good date from going bad. It may seem obvious, but the even the smallest overlooked detail can spoil a date. If you get heartburn during a meal, you may focus on your discomfort instead of your candidate. If you underestimate the cost of your date and can't find a cash machine, you may end up "doing dishes" rather than "doing the town." "Be prepared" is not only the Boy Scout motto – it's the love recruiter's motto too! Bring with you on all dates:

- ♥ A cellular phone (or a phone card and a few quarters for a pay phone)
- ♥ The phone number of friend (dating buddy) who will be home to take your call if you need help
- ♥ The phone numbers of a few reliable car services

- ♥ A roll of antacid tablets and a packet of bromide salts
- ♥ Condoms
- ♥ At least $20 in "mad money"

Mad About "Mad Money"

We believe the term "mad money" was first coined by wives who secretly squirreled away bits of the household allowance for an extravagant extra (which anyone would have to be "mad" to buy). You might also recall Mom pressing a few dollars into your hand before your big date, saying: "Here's mad money, just in case." Both of you hoped you wouldn't be spending it, because mad money was to be used **only** if you were in trouble.

For adults, mad money still serves the same purpose. You might need it for transportation if you get "mad" at your date, or s/he gets mad at you and leaves you stranded. Each time you go out you should carry at least $20 that you don't plan to spend — you just never know when you'll need it for a situation you didn't plan on. (Perhaps to help pay a unusually large check.)

Planning your Mental and Verbal Icebreakers

On a job interview, you have only one chance to make a good first impression. How you look, what you say and how you act in the first few moments will seal your fate before you ever talk about your skills. It's the same with recruiting love, but unfortunately, those first few moments are also the most awkward. How friendly should you be and what can you say that doesn't make you sound totally corny or nervous? You're not ready to interview your candidates until you've given some thought to your initial approach. Along with the tools we've described for your dating kit, we suggest you tuck a few prepared "icebreakers" in as well.

When two people meet, one of them must "break the ice" with a look, a smile or a comment. How you choose to initiate contact depends on your own personal style. Nelson is an extremely outgoing person who greets everyone with a joke. This works for him, because telling jokes makes Nelson feel very confident and, good or bad, his jokes are usually rewarded with a smile. However, most of us wouldn't feel comfortable breaking the ice with: "Did you hear the one about the man who walks into the bar carrying a duck?"

You already know that direct eye contact, a warm smile, an extended hand, and a simple "hello," will get you through the first 20 seconds of almost any first encounter. It's the *next* 20 seconds that stump many people. Try making comments about your surroundings or the activity you've chosen, as in:

- ♥ "Thanks for coming out here to meet me. I think you'll love the Mexican coffee — let's sit over there?"

- ♥ "I'm really glad we could get together. I really am looking forward to getting to know you better."

If you're not a spontaneous talker, it might help you to prepare some general topics (politics, current events, even the weather) beforehand for times when the conversation lags. Are you both movie buffs? Mention the movies you've seen recently and ask your date if s/he's seen them too. Ask about her/his reaction? Did s/he say that s/he's thinking of buying a new car? If you've studied up on some of the new models or about the ratings in *Consumer Reports*, the evening will whiz by as you

Nice to meet you, so, did you hear the one about the man who walks into a bar carrying a duck?

debate the pros and cons of each car. Of course, you'll also want to talk about each other. Just remember not to divulge too many deeply personal details.

As openers get easier for you, it may be tempting to get creative. This is fine, but keep in mind that the purpose of an opening line isn't to be memorable; it's to open the door of communication. Cutesy, sexist, insulting or confusing opening lines will put the recipient off-guard, make them uncomfortable instead of receptive, and may even repulse them. To give you a better idea of what we mean, here are some of the very worst lines that people have used on us:

- "Hey baby, what's your sign?"
- "Waiting for Godot?"
- "It took me over two long hours in traffic to get here!"
- "My place or yours?"
- "Isn't this place/club/activity/organization stupid? I never do this type of thing."

If you want to make your first approach more memorable, call attention to yourself in a positive way. Wear eye-catching jewelry or a funky hat. Carry an interesting book with you, but don't bury your head in it!

Your Dating Log: The Key to Your Success

In Chapter 5, you learned about the importance of your dating log as a key to a focused, organized search, but it will also help you impress everyone you meet.

Since you started your job as a love recruiter, you've probably been meeting more people than usual. Your impressions and specific details about each candidate may become fuzzy without a carefully kept log. After every date, Lars always forgot details like candidates' last names, phone numbers, and other things he really wanted to remember. He was hesitant when we suggested that he carry a little pad to make notes while his date was in the restroom, or in his car before he went home. Later, Lars reported that his dating log system was running smoothly and his little note pad had made him more efficient in general, as he'd also begun to write down notes on other things he used to forget!

If you have exchanged cards with someone, make a few notes on the back of his/her card about what impressed you. If you don't get a card, make notes on the back of your own card, in a little notebook like Lars, or in a pinch, even on a paper towel in the restroom. When you get home, don't forget to enter this information in your dating log. She's allergic to seafood? You won't make the mistake of taking her to the Rusty Barnacle because you forgot! He loves classical music? You'll score points when you suggest the free concert in the park next week.

As you get to know one another, your dating log will swell with information on your candidates. They'll be impressed when, again and again, you mention bits of information or talk about subjects that s/he never thought you knew. You'll be able to surprise your candidate with a card on Groundhog Day (his favorite holiday) even though he just mentioned it in passing a few months ago. When she finally comes for dinner and you serve *magret de canard*, she'll be amazed that you picked the dish she loved best when visiting Paris last summer. You'll hear "how did you **know**?" over and over again! You can't fake interest in someone for long without being exposed as a fraud, however, just like the good salesman who remembers your birthday, remembering what has meaning to a person, and following up on it, is a surefire way to impress! (His grandmother loves Pavarotti; she likes yellow roses the most; his toddler likes the red Power Ranger, etc.) Politicians, executives, and others who constantly interface with the public use this technique to personalize conversations and make the other person feel special and important. Maybe your dating log won't become a bestseller, but it will be the most fascinating and important document you'll ever create during your love search.

Fashion Tools

Many a love recruiter would return that expensive outfit if s/he knew the candidate didn't even notice it, because the candidate was focusing on other things! Having said this, what you wear does, to some extent, have a positive or negative influence on your candidate. In business, wearing the wrong clothes for a job interview can mean disaster. Who will take you seriously if you show up for that financial analyst interview in shorts and a T-shirt? And, if you wear a business suit to that lifeguard interview, you'll also raise a few eyebrows.

I Thought You Said It Was a Casual Place!

Fashion used to have hard and fast rules: don't wear white before Memorial Day or after Labor Day, a woman's outfit isn't complete without gloves, a man's outfit isn't complete without a hat, etc. We rebelled against these fashion restraints, but the freedom can be confusing at times. Who hasn't appeared in jeans, only to discover everyone else in business or evening clothes?

What you wear and how you carry it off does have a lot to do with your success in love, life and business, but you don't have to be a *Vogue* or *GQ* fashion editor to dress appropriately for a date. The most important things to keep in mind are:

- ♥ Wear clothing that makes you look and feel normal and comfortable.
- ♥ If possible, find out in advance where you're going and what you're doing and wear clothing appropriate for the activity and the weather.

If you are seriously going to recruit love, you'll need clothes appropriate to a variety of different situations. At the elegant Rainbow Room in New York City, dressing appropriately will take on an entirely different meaning from your date at Wild Water Kingdom! And it doesn't make much sense to wear high heels instead of sneakers on a walking tour, or a light jacket on a cold day, even if they do look best with your outfit.

Business Attire "Works" For Recruiting Love

Savvy job seekers know that the right uniform for a job interview is usually the business suit, or a close variation. In the working world, a suit is still considered the "uniform" of power, status, and good taste. Since recruiting love is a lot like job hunting, standard business attire is usually a safe choice if you're not sure what to wear. Many of your recruiting activities will probably occur right after work, anyway. Men can take off their tie and jacket, and women can dress up their business suit with a few accessories. If you're caught in a situation that calls for extremely casual or dressy clothes and you're dressed in work clothes, you can always say you had a long day at the office, and didn't have time to change. Men who can't stand the idea of wearing a suit can wear a sport jacket, nicely tailored pants, and a shirt and tie. Women can usually count on a well-tailored jacket with a skirt or pants, worn with a silky blouse.

Formal events take a little more planning, but there's no need to panic! You don't have to turn down a black tie invitation because you don't want to run out and buy a tuxedo or evening gown. Men can get by with a dark business suit, well-polished dress shoes, a solid color shirt, and a conservative tie. Women can usually manage a dressy enough look in a good quality business dress, a suit with a silky blouse and sparkly accessories, or a long skirt with a dressy blouse. Under no circumstances should a woman wear a conspicuously sexy gown or cocktail dress unless she is sure her date won't be embarrassed by all the attention she is likely to get.

> Tina said:
> I was so excited when Kevin invited me to his company's annual dinner dance that I spent a month's salary on a designer gown with a dramatic plunging neckline and practically no back. It was stunning — sure to draw the attention of everyone in the room. I was the one who was stunned! When I took off my coat at the hotel, Kevin's reaction was less than enthusiastic — he insisted that I wear his jacket most of the evening!

When you go shopping, keep in mind that while men and women may ogle sexy models in magazines, most people are uncomfortable being out in public with someone who is dressed in an outfit so outrageous that s/he becomes the center of attention.

What about the times when revealing your body is expected? Susan turned down a romantic weekend in the Caribbean because she didn't want to reveal herself in a bathing suit or shorts. All of us have aspects of our bodies that we'd rather hide, or swap for something better. Your feelings about your body should not stop you from having a good time! You're probably more critical than anyone else, but if you're really self-conscious, you can wear a long, loose t-shirt over your bathing suit or shorts. This will cover you up without making you look absurd. Of course, if you've thought for some time that your body can use some improvement, maybe this is the time to stop procrastinating and "just do it." You know you're worth it!

Marketing Your Self-Image

What do you clothes say about you? Are you a classic person who enjoys the sleek line of well-tailored clothes? The outdoors type who appreciates well-crafted hiking boots and functional sweaters? A true romantic in velvet, silk, and lace? A cowboy type who would never be caught without boots and a Stetson? The list of "types" is as infinite as the many facets of your personality. You can dress in many different ways, and feel good in them all, depending on the day and the circumstances. No matter what image you choose to project with your clothes, keep these basic rules in mind:

- ♥ No matter what you wear, there is never any excuse for appearing dirty, sloppy, or badly groomed!

- ♥ Don't alter your personal style in a way that makes you uncomfortable just because someone else would like you to look that way.

♥ Make sure your image isn't grossly outdated, and that you're not conveying signals that you don't mean to. (An image review is part of your "Action Memo" for this chapter.)

I Wore This to My High School Prom Everyone Said I Looked Great!

Many adults continue to maintain a "look" long after it stops being fashionable. What was once the height of fashion might just look **odd** today. If you haven't made any major adjustments to your hair or clothes in years, you're probably due for an image update. You're also due for an image makeover if your personal style has been immobile since 1954. It's great that you can still fit into your army uniform or prom dress — but that doesn't mean you should wear them now!

Image consultants help people put their "best foot forward," but enlisting professional, personalized service can be very expensive. If you're basically happy with the way you look, you can do a mini-image-analysis and makeover yourself: Start by looking at current magazines, movies, and television shows. How are people of your own age group dressing? Do you appear very different? Recruit a trusted, impartial friend (Preferably one with good taste!) to help you analyze your wardrobe, accessories, makeup and hairstyle. Ask him/her to be candid. Do your clothes project your personality, your socio-economic status, your intelligence level, your career and romance goals? Marnie attended a wardrobe workshop at her local *Alternative University* because she wanted her relationships with the wealthy businessmen she was recruiting to extend beyond dinner and invitations to the bedroom:

I always wear my prom dress when I really want to make an impression!

> Marnie said:
> The image consultants suggested that I swap the bright makeup and funky, body-hugging clothes I usually wore, for conservative but well-designed dresses, soft suits with silk blouses, and interesting scarves and jewelry. I was afraid that I wouldn't get noticed in clothes like that, but I seemed to meet more qualified candidates than ever before!

When you shop for new clothes, or invest in a new hairstyle or accessories, remember that recruiting love is an investment that you're making in yourself. If your budget can't handle all these expenses at once, prioritize them based on immediate need, and perhaps just borrow a few things to update your existing wardrobe. Sometimes, you can give new life to some garments just by widening or narrowing a lapel, lengthening or shortening a hem, or adding a scarf or tie.

We hope that you will be loved for what's *in* your head, but don't forget the hair that covers it! Is your hairstyle a remnant of earlier generations or just plain unflattering? Take time to examine other aspects of your image that could turn potential candidates off. If you are still unhappy about your appearance after your own mini make-over, consider calling a professional. A certified image consultant can suggest flattering colors, hairstyles, accessories, makeup, wardrobe, etc. Some consultants will even go shopping with you. The result will be a look designed just for you which maximizes your best features and makes you look your best.

THE BOTTOM LINE

"Beware of all enterprises that require new clothes."
Henry David Thoreau

From the desk of: The Advice Sisters

TO: *You Company* Recruiter

FROM: Alison and Jessica

RE: Summary of Chapter 6:
Tools to Facilitate the Search

1. Some essential tools for recruiting love are:

   - ♥ An answering machine
   - ♥ An etiquette book
   - ♥ Personal cards
   - ♥ A dating kit
   - ♥ Some pre-rehearsed verbal ice-breakers
   - ♥ Your dating log
   - ♥ A business suit or dress (for first dates)
   - ♥ An appropriate wardrobe for your activities

2. Image appraisals are important to a love recruiter's success: conduct a mini make-over or enlist the aid of a professional.

Summary Blueprint

From the desk of: The Advice Sisters

Today's Date: _____

1. Get an answering machine, voice mail, or an answering service if necessary.

I will complete this by: _____

2. Order your personal cards, assemble your "dating kit" and arrange for a "dating buddy."

I will complete this by: _____

3. Choose a few locations for your first dates, and prepare and practice ice breakers if necessary.

I will complete this by: _____

4. Evaluate your wardrobe and image. If you need help, consult a friend or professional.

I will complete this by: _____

5. Buy or borrow an etiquette book and read it.

I will complete this by: _____

6. Go on to Chapter 7.

I will complete this by: _____

148   Recruiting Love

And then at 14 months, I had an ear infection that persisted for two weeks.

From the desk of: The Advice Sisters

TO: *You Company* Recruiter

FROM: Alison and Jessica

RE: Chapter 7:
        Improving Your "Interviewing Skills"

In this chapter, you will learn how to put the *You Company's* best foot forward to help you attract the finest candidates for the *You Company* search. We'll give you strategies and tips for handling a variety of interview situations, both good and bad.

15-Second Memo

You probably don't even realize it (it's so second-nature) but every day at work you follow certain unwritten "rules of behavior." These rules have helped you function in society, make good impressions, and move up the career ladder.

What exactly do we mean by "rules of behavior?" Let's use the example of a business meeting. If you're holding the meeting, you develop an agenda, establish a time and place, and reserve a room. The participants mark the time and place on their calendar, and carefully review the agenda beforehand. The day of the meeting, everyone arrives on time, with all the materials they need to actively participate. Everyone knows they must be diplomatic — even if there are strong differences of opinion — because business meetings are "civil" forums. When was the last time you saw fists fly at a business meeting?

In Chapter 6 we told you how to improve your image, but looking good won't cancel out poor behavior. You have to know how to prepare, act and take control of the recruiting process.

What do we mean by good dating behavior? It's more than good manners — although they're essential too. (People who lick their fingers or push ahead in line will never make it onto anyone's list of top candidates.) How you handle dating stress, ensure safety, and display consideration, will all affect the outcome of your search.

This chapter will show some dating dilemmas and sticky situations that you're likely to face. We'll help you to become a more talented recruiter by helping you improve your interviewing skills.

How Much Do You Tell?

When you were a child you were probably told: "Don't talk to strangers." It's still good advice, however, everyone you meet for the first time is a stranger until you get to know them better! And the only good way to get to know them better is by talking to them!

Savvy love recruiters act **with caution!** It's almost impossible to judge the character and motives of someone you've just met. Of course you can't keep your lips totally sealed and make any new contacts; however, "Tell me about yourself" at a first or second encounter should not include any personal particulars. As in a job interview, some things should initially be kept to yourself. Never reveal intimate details about your personal wealth, or health. You might tell someone new that you've recently separated, but the exact details of the settlement, or that you've had a nervous breakdown over it, are best left for later. Questions like: "Where do you live?" or: "Where do you work?" should be answered with: "I live in Pleasantville," or "I work Downtown." Never give someone you've just met your exact home or work address, even if you're introduced through a mutual friend.

> Billy said:
> I met Janis at a party through a friend. I thought we might get together, so I gave her my home address and phone number. We did go out once, but afterwards I called her and said that I didn't think we should see each other again.
> Janis wouldn't take no for an answer. She left dozens of calls on my answering machine, and some of them were pretty wild.

> About a month after I met her, Janis showed up on my doorstep just as a date and I were going out. She was carrying a bouquet of flowers and a bottle of wine. When I gently told her again that I wasn't interested, she screamed and threw both the flowers and the wine at my door. Several neighbors stuck their heads out windows to see what all the commotion was about. I felt bad for her, but I was really embarrassed for my date.

You don't have to be unfriendly; just save the personal details until you know the person well.

> ▶ Irene said:
> I'm a successful entrepreneur and a small-town celebrity of sorts. At a political fundraiser, a man I didn't recognize made a beeline for me. Brian told me that he was in advertising, and just in town for a few days. When he asked me out to dinner, I immediately accepted.
>
> Brian seemed really interested, and wanted to know everything about me. I'm usually more cautious with first encounters but after several glasses of wine, I told him some very personal things.
>
> A few days later an dismayed friend called to tell me that on page 2 of the paper was a "tell-all" story about the *Real Irene Thurgood,* and it included all the personal details that I had told Brian at dinner!
>
> It didn't take a rocket scientist to figure out that Brian was a reporter, prepared to do whatever it took (even pretending to be romantically interested in me) to get a story.

Safety Begins at Home

Billy and Irene's problems may seem obvious to you, but safety is probably the most overlooked aspect of adult dating. We can't stress this enough — be careful with a new candidate, no matter how small and close knit your community, or how honest your new candidate appears. The Boston Strangler was an educated, well dressed, good looking man and everyone thought he was "such a nice boy."

So, for the first few "interviews," tell your date you'd feel more comfortable arranging your own transportation and meeting in a public place. Even if your date says: "it's no trouble" to pick you up, firmly refuse the offer. Anyone who doesn't understand and respect your feelings about this should ring some warning bells. The whole purpose of *Recruiting Love* is to bypass such toads. If you must be picked up, meet your date outside at the curb; DO NOT let him/her into your home.

Once you're out on a date, don't leave your car and accept a ride anywhere else. Rikki followed our advice and took her own car, but didn't follow her safety plan all the way through:

> Rikki said:
> On my second date with Randy, he suggested that we go to a disco after dinner. He said I should leave my car in the restaurant parking lot (and go in his car) because it was tough to park at the disco. He'd bring me back to my car later.
> After a few minutes I realized that we were heading in the wrong direction! When I mentioned this to Randy, he crooned: "but baby, my place is so much more intimate, and my roommate's gone

> for the weekend!" I asked him to either go to the disco or take me back to my car. Suddenly, he pulled sharply over to the side of the road, unlocked the doors, and motioned me out. Then he sped away, tires squealing. I had to walk alone in the dark to a phone booth. Luckily, I had the number of a friend and quarters for the phone so I could get back to my car.

The point is: if you don't want to end up at your date's house, at "Inspiration Point," or somewhere else you don't want to be, use common sense, keep control, and stay safe. Here are a few other "safety pointers" you might not automatically think of:

- ♥ Get Directions! (you too, men!) A late date, a frazzled date, or a "completely lost" date, isn't a romantic date!

- ♥ If you're taking public transportation, make sure it runs late enough for you to get home, especially if you decide to "paint the town."

- ♥ Be certain your transportation works. Many a nice date has been ruined sitting on a highway waiting for the road service, or for a train that never comes. Have enough gas in your car, or a bus or train schedule if you take public transportation.

Interview Candidates at Your "Office"

When you go for a job interview, you go to the interviewer's turf (usually his/her office). Follow the same principle for your love interviews, especially first dates. Ask your candidates to meet you somewhere you go often (your "office"). If you go somewhere familiar,

Improving Your Interviewing Skills 155

I KNEW we should have made a right at that third cliff! Hey you, up there with the feathers, how do you get to the clam festival?

you'll also know what the date will cost (especially important if you're paying the whole bill, or sharing the check). Most people will appreciate an enthusiastic suggestion — so enthuse about the sumptuous desserts at your local coffee bar, or the great salad bar at your favorite restaurant. Your candidate doesn't have to know that you're thinking about your comfort and safety.

There are more good reasons for meeting in public places. Not every date turns out to be the stuff dreams are made of. If the conversation lags, you can always point out the huge man with two dinner plates sitting with the small woman with a tiny salad, or comment on the strolling guitarist who is strumming: "I Love Paris" in front of the arguing couple!

Who Pays?

Gone are the days when a date automatically meant that the man paid. In the 90s, woman are doing the asking a lot more often, and are also expected to pay their share of expenses. If you haven't dated for a while, this may take some getting used to, but on the whole, we think sharing expenses is a good thing. Adult partners have an equal stake in the date, and it does away with the line:

> "Hey, I showed you a good time and bought you dinner, so what are you going to do for me?"

Having said all this, the question of who pays can still be sticky. If you want to go dutch (each partner pays his/her own) that should be decided **before** the date.

> Joe said:
> Carol selected the fanciest restaurant in town, but since she'd asked me out I said okay. Carol knew I was between jobs, but she was a senior executive and could easily afford it.
> We both enjoyed dinner, and then the check came. The server put it in the middle of the table and there it sat, both of us staring at it. Finally, with an irritated sigh, Carol grabbed it, looked at it for a split second, and then said: "You drank most of that bottle of wine, but just give me a hundred bucks and we'll call it even."
> I was flabbergasted. She'd asked me out, she'd selected the place, and she knew I couldn't afford a hundred-dollar meal. "Carol," I said. "I'm embarrassed to say this but you know I'm between jobs and I don't have that kind of cash." "No problem," she said. "There's a cash machine down the block. I could have another coffee while I wait."

The simple question: "Are we going dutch on this one?" would have avoided this mess. For first dates, the general rule is just like in business: the one who does the inviting is expected to pay. If you're a man who can't accept a woman paying your tab, or if you're a woman who doesn't like a man to pick up the bill, offer to pay half, or even all. Some dates will be flattered and accept, but others may refuse. If this bothers you, say: "Okay, this'll be yours, but the next time it's on me." After you've been dating awhile you'll probably alternate the expenses anyway (or reciprocate with concert tickets, a home-cooked meal, etc.).

Make Your Friends Part of Your Date! (We Mean It!)

By now you know you have to be cautious about safety on the first few dates. We like the idea of "dating buddies." Before your date, tell your "buddy" who you're seeing and where you're going. Arrange to call him/her by a certain time after the date, and agree that if you don't, s/he will follow up to make sure that you're okay. This isn't much of a hardship, because most love recruiters like to call a friend after a date, anyway.

> Laura said:
> After a couple of dates with Dave, all in public places, I accepted a dinner invitation at his house. We had a good time until I got up to leave. Then, Dave's charming manner abruptly vanished. He blocked the door and said I could only leave when HE was ready to let me go!
> I should've been frightened, but I sensed that Dave was just bullying me. I calmly informed him that I'd given his address and phone number to my friend Sally, and that she was calling me around midnight. If I didn't answer, Sally was to call the police and give them Dave's address and phone number.
> As I'd speculated, Dave backed off. He even called me the next day! My response? I chucked Dave right back into the toad pond!

The Date is Over — Now What?

We've already said that during your first few dates you should not let anyone into your home at the beginning of the evening. It's also not a good idea to let them in at the end. (When the relationship is further advanced and you want your date to stay, this obviously won't be an issue anymore.) So what do you do if it's late, you're together, and your date insists on walking you to your door? Or wants coffee? Or a nightcap?

The rule of thumb is always: don't agree to it unless you want to. If you live in an apartment building, you can avoid confrontation by walking to the lobby and saying your farewells there. If you live where there is no front door other than your own, stop at the curb, or in your driveway — not in front of the door — hold your house keys in your hand, and say:

> "Thanks for a lovely time. If you wouldn't mind, I'd really appreciate if you'd watch from here to make sure no one is around while I get inside."

Most people will get the message that they are not going to get an invitation to come in.

And what about sharing a kiss goodnight? Whether you are a man or a woman, you are never obligated to give any kind of sexual favors (even a kiss) just because you agreed to a date. If you don't want to kiss your date goodnight (or anything else) just say "no thanks."

Perhaps you're now at the point where you'd to spend a little more time with your date, but you're not ready for an overnight guest. Don't invite your date in unless you are prepared to address how long the person will stay. We don't want to scare you, but the subject of "date rape" has been all over the news. You may have heard horrible stories about people who thought they knew their date well enough to feel safe.

Even when you're sure you want to invite someone into your home, you may still face some awkward situations. What do you do if your otherwise-nice candidate has overstayed his/her welcome? Just stand up, get your date's coat and say:

> "This has been fun, but it's really getting late and I have an important obligation early in the morning. I'll bet you need to get some sleep too."

It's corny, but it works (most of the time). Experience has shown us, however, that some people may not get the hint. You may need to repeat yourself more firmly. If you are *still* ignored, **open the door**, stand to the side and say in a friendly but absolutely firm manner:

> "I mean it. Last call is over. I'd like you to go home."

Anyone who continues to resist is obviously going to be a real problem. There are some aggressive types who think they can force the issue if they hold out long enough — but you don't have to allow that! Link arms with your date, move directly into your open doorway, and while nudging him or her forward, say:

> "Look, I had a good time tonight (if you did) but I'm not ready for you to stay over. Let's not ruin a good thing. Please leave."

We hope it never gets to the point that you fear for your own safety and have to call the police or leave and get help. Usually, stubborn holdouts are harmless — just socially inept and testing your patience.

> Cindy said:
> Rick and I were on our fourth cup of coffee, and he showed no signs of leaving. I liked him, but I wasn't ready to spend the night with him. I tried everything to get him to leave, but he remained rooted to my couch. I wasn't afraid of him, but I didn't want him to stay. Finally, I stood up and said: "Rick, if you want to spend the night here go ahead, but I need my sleep and I'm going to go into my bedroom — alone — and I'm locking the door. So, see you in the morning." He got the message at that point!

Savvy, Safe Sex

It's a big leap from a goodnight kiss to a night of romance, but we're assuming that at some point you'll want to do more than just hold hands. Only you and your partner will know what, when, where, and how. There is only one rule here: **NEVER have sex to be accommodating, and NEVER have unprotected sex for ANY reason!** Anyone who insists upon sex as a show of love gets an immediate rejection notice and a one-way ticket back to the toad pond!

Unless you're Rip Van Winkle and haven't kept up with world events due to a long sleep, you know that AIDS can kill you. Other social diseases can ruin your social life for a long, long time. And if you're recruiting love, it's certainly not the right time to create a new life! Your job is to recruit love, not disaster! You may think your judgement is far too good for you to be carried away on an unanticipated sea of passion, but even the most sensible people can surprise themselves. For this reason, you should always carry condoms on every date;

never rely on someone else to take care of it. It's too late to worry about the results of spontaneous, unprotected sex after it's over.

I Can't Remember What I Did Last Night!

Although many people use alcohol and drugs to relax and loosen up, overuse can sabotage your search. You might end up in a compromising position without remembering how you got there. How will you or your date ever know if you are right for each other if you can't remember what either of you said or did? Getting "wasted" may be partying for some, but it's just a "waste" for you, the serious love recruiter.

Handling Dating Disasters – When Bad Dates Happen to Good People

Sometimes even the most promising dates go wrong. If you're following the *Recruiting Love* plan, your careful attention to planning should lessen your quotient of bad dates. Life isn't 100% predictable, however, so into your life a few bad dates may fall! Sometimes, the chemistry isn't right, or one of you has had a bad day. Sometimes, external factors (weather, car problems, bad news, etc.) turn an otherwise nice date into a bad one. Of course, you might just have misjudged your candidate who just turns out to be a "jerk." Chalk it up to experience, and move on.

If you control your dating situations with planning, common sense and quick thinking, you can avoid many situations leading to dating disaster.

Plan Ahead

Successful business meetings start with good planning. It's the same with a good date.

You can't plan for every contingency, but you can think about your date in general terms. Consider what kind of date you'll be going on, and tell your candidate (or ask him/her) what the plan will be before you actually meet. Is your date a vegetarian? Don't pick the steakhouse. Allergic to fur? Your date won't stop sneezing long enough hold a conversation at the cat show! Afraid of heights? It won't be a relaxing evening if his/her knees are knocking in that mile-high revolving restaurant. If you're going out to eat, at least ask about food preferences. If you're planning anything that requires special clothing (horseback riding, tennis, visiting the cattle auction) let your date know ahead of time. If your idea of an exciting date is slam dancing at a punk nightclub, the cock fights, or a swing club, don't be thoughtless enough to suggest such activities unless you're sure your date finds them acceptable. If your date suggests something unacceptable, speak up! You'll save both of you a lot of embarrassment and distress.

Abusive Dates

We hope you're not going to suffer through any truly bad dates, but there are ways to handle them. Let's go back to our business meeting analogy.

We said that everyone involved in a meeting has unspoken responsibilities and rules of conduct (be on time, come prepared, be civil, etc.). In a love search, whether you're the recruiter or the candidate, you also have responsibilities and rules (be on time, be involved, be pleasant, etc.). Your candidates will probably follow most of these rules, but occasionally you'll find someone who just doesn't have any social graces. If your date acts inconsiderate, insulting, embarrassing or abusive, point out that if s/he doesn't stop it you will leave — and then follow through if necessary!

> Phyllis said:
> I had been really looking forward to my first date with Arthur. When we first met he seemed sweet, and really interested in what I had to say. Unfortunately, at the restaurant Arthur turned from Dr. Jekyll into Mr. Hyde. No matter what I said, Arthur disagreed. He even challenged my dinner order, saying my choice of lasagna showed I had no class. He criticized everything about me — my opinions, my looks, my politics, even my choice of words! At the end of the meal, I moved to pick up the check (I'd asked for the date) and he snatched it away from me. As he held it triumphantly aloft I said, "You know, when I'm out with someone I like, I let them pay for me — but in your case, please tell me exactly what I owe!"

And here's another story, with a great twist!

> Alice said:
> My mother's friend fixed me up with the son of a friend of hers. He was a doctor, never married, and recently moved to town.
> Chad called me, and without a lengthy conversation (he was on call at the hospital) asked me to the movie. He arrived wearing dirty jeans and a stained, wrinkled shirt. His car was equally

dirty, and he drove like a maniac all the way to the theater. Once inside, he raced us past the popcorn and up to the first row, where the speakers were blaring and the screen was blurry.

Afterwards, Chad drove me straight home, again, like a maniac. I don't think we exchanged more than two words the entire evening. Clearly, he'd been talked into this date, as I had, but it wasn't fair of him to take it out on me! "I'll call you Tuesday," Chad mumbled as he sped off.

Well, I'd been a victim long enough! I decided that when Chad called I'd tell him what I should have told lots of awful dates before him: that he wasn't nice, we didn't have anything in common, and I didn't want him to call me ever again!

The following Tuesday, I was working at home, waiting for the window washer, when the phone rang: "Hello?" It was Chad's voice! I launched right into my rehearsed speech: "Look Chad, we have absolutely nothing in common. I don't want to see you and I don't want you to call here again." Then I slammed the phone down! I felt great! I'd told him off just as I promised myself.

The window washer never arrived that day, so I called on Wednesday to find out why. "Well," said the woman who answered the phone, "He DID call, but someone there told him never to call again." And in that instant I realized — I hadn't told off Chad—I'd told off the window washer!

My Date is More Like a Dud than a Dream!

Most of your candidates will not be abusive like Alice's or Phyllis's. You'll have met them in person (except for blind dates or dates through personal ads and dating services) and you selected them because they met your basic qualifications. Even so, it can be a very long evening when one or both of you misjudged the fit and you're not having a good time. Must you go through with the date?

Think back to when you were interviewing for jobs. Weren't there times when either you or the interviewer knew right away that there wasn't a match? Yet the interviewer still met with you out of courtesy, and you went through with it for the same reasons. At work, you'd never just walk out of a discussion with your boss just because it wasn't pleasurable. When you're recruiting love, the same courtesy should be extended to your candidates.

If your dream candidate turns out to be a dud, you will need some way to allow both of you to save face while you extricate yourself gracefully. It's usually better to create a "little fib" rather than come right out and hurt someone's feelings with the absolute truth. It's far better to end a disappointing-but-not-dangerous date with a harmless excuse than by abruptly stating: "This date stinks and I'm not having fun so I'm just going to leave right now!" Both of you are already disappointed — why hurt someone's feelings too? Try some variation of the following "traditional" excuses — they may be just what you need to get through an awkward experience:

- ♥ Tell your candidate you're working on a big project and you have to call your office. Make the "call," and then leave with apologies.
- ♥ Call home and "discover" a "family emergency." Leave immediately, with apologies.

♥ Tell your candidate that you're really not feeling well and you're sorry, but you must cut the date short. Who can prove you're not sick?

A job interviewer rarely rejects a candidate to his/her face at an interview, and you should extend the same consideration to a candidate. The best way to tell someone you don't want to see them again is over the phone.

What's Taboo on a First Date?

We've said that in both love and business interviews you shouldn't divulge super-personal details. Your ex-romances or your prior sex life are **definitely** taboo subjects on a first date. Save all those funny, sad, and embarrassing personal stories for when you're better acquainted. If you've just been through a breakup, your new candidate doesn't need to hear the details.

> Sandra said:
> I was looking forward to dating Gary, even though he told me that he'd recently broken up with his long-time girlfriend. However, he'd assured me that he was over her and ready to try again.
> Our date started off fine, but over dinner Gary began to talk about his ex-girlfriend — and he talked — and talked. Soon, he was blubbering uncontrollably into his napkin and we had to leave.
> When Gary called the next day I told him I didn't think he was ready to see anyone new. I really liked Gary, and I knew he'd make a good candidate someday, but what would be the point of going out with him now?

Taboo on Any Date: The Big Six

There are so many ways to sabotage an otherwise good date that we could write an entire amusing-but-horrifying book of these stories. However, there are six dating mistakes that even the sophisticated recruiter can make:

1. Being A Good Sport Against Common Sense

If you get seasick and your date wants to go sailing, don't keep silent to be a good sport. You may end up greener than the sea! If you're a couch potato and your date suggests a strenuous hike through the mountains, speak up — nothing ruins a date faster than passing out on the trail. Kindly but firmly suggest an alternative.

> ▶ Arlene said:
> Fred invited me to dinner at the beach, and afterwards, we walked along the boardwalk. Fred saw that thing that turns you upside down and swings you around by your feet and he wanted us to ride it. My heart sank. We'd just eaten a huge dinner — just thinking about being on that ride turned me green — I get sick on short car trips! But I really liked Fred and I wanted to be a good sport, so I agreed to go. I didn't even make it halfway through the ride before I got violently ill. As we cleaned up, Fred angrily said: "We didn't have to ride — why didn't you just tell me that you get sick on those rides!" It was the last date we ever had and it was really my fault — I should have been honest.

2. Making False Claims

Sure, you'd like to impress your date, but not at the risk of being foolish. Before you brag about something, make sure you can follow through. Here are just a few examples of false claims that recruiters have used to impress candidates:

- ♥ Saying they can dance, cook, etc. when they can't
- ♥ Offering to get sold-out show tickets when they can't
- ♥ Saying they know people they don't
- ♥ Saying they're wealthy when they're not
- ♥ Claiming contacts they don't have
- ♥ Claiming false family connections or titles

3. Not Asking about Values and Lifestyles

We can't stress this enough. What's natural for you may not be comfortable for someone else.

> ▶ Jonathan said:
> Meg and I had been dating for a while, and I was looking forward to the dinner she offered to make at her house. When I got there her place was a mess! I looked around for our dinner, but the only possible eating space — her kitchen table — was littered with papers, books, and clothes. "Sit right there," she said cheerfully, pointing to a lumpy couch where her gigantic golden retriever was lying. Then Meg opened a can of chili & beans, scooped it into three bowls, and presented one of them to me — and one to the dog! I made

This is so much better than that dinner theatre cruise.

> some excuse to leave, and laughed all the way home. She should have at least called for a pizza!

For Meg, eating on the couch and sharing her dinner with the dog was normal behavior. Jonathan was horrified! He usually enjoyed gourmet food and good wine — and he never even let his dog eat table scraps!

The point of all this:

Be aware of possible differences between the two of you when you plan a date — and ask first!

4. Getting Drunk, Wild, or Out-of-Control

Even if "Animal House" is your idea of an ideal evening, don't subject your new date to that atmosphere. It's absolutely unacceptable to get drunk or out of control, even if it's what you really feel like doing. If you know alcohol can get the better of you, business rules apply: Drink moderately or not at all. We know a businessman who orders a brandy or similar "sipping drink" and holds it all night. We've also heard of people who tip a bartender at a party, restaurant, or bar NOT to put more than a dollop of liquor in their drinks, no matter how many they order. And, of course, it's completely acceptable to just have mineral water. Many adults now do this anyway, just to "cut down on the calories."

If your date drinks too much or gets out of control, try to get him/her away from the source of the trouble. Don't allow your date to drive if s/he has been drinking all night. If the person resists or gets belligerent in public, ask for help. If you're alone and the situation gets bad enough, call the Police, then leave.

5. Subjecting Your Date to Family and Friends Too Soon

In sitcoms, no one dreams of getting seriously involved with anyone who hasn't passed muster with the wacky, zany and all-important group of friends. In real life, it's pretty much the same, and you can be sure that there will be instances when your friends don't "love the one you're with." This is even more true for family. The same mother who constantly bugged you to "go out and meet somebody nice" suddenly develops standards that the world's most perfect person couldn't meet. We know a man whose family and close friends hated his fiancee so much that they tried to talk him out marrying her at the wedding, and failing that, cried forlornly during the ceremony and throughout the reception!

At some point you'll want to (and have to) introduce your "new love" to your friends and family. Our advice: Resist the urge until you're sure you'll be seeing this person for a while. Did your mother adore your former sweetheart, or was she just getting used to him/her when you announced your breakup? We've already told you that first impressions are hard to shake — so do your best to make the first meeting pleasant. If it's done poorly, the newcomer may get the cold shoulder or the third degree.

> Linda said:
> Jack took to me to a wedding on our fourth date. I didn't know anyone, but most of the guests were friends of Jack's and his ex-wife, Lynn. Before Jack had a chance to introduce me, people came up to him and said, "Jack, you're looking terrific — where's Lynn? Then before he could answer they'd turn to me and confidentially say: "Have you met Lynn yet? She's so great — they should really get back together!" I felt terrible. Needless to say, we don't see a lot of those friends now that Jack and I are living together.

We know that friends and family care about you and, therefore, they are sometimes overly protective. So wait until your relationship is strong enough to survive any pressure brought on by your loved ones.

6. Mixing Pleasure with Business too Soon

The right person can brighten your evening and enhance your image in your company's eyes by charming your boss and colleagues. The wrong date can make you the target of office jokes, or worse. If you plan to invite a date to a business function, know who you're dealing with (including that person's social habits) before you mix business with pleasure. Many a mild-mannered date has gotten out of hand and rowdily "entertained" someone's boss at a cocktail party. (And what was that about the promotion you were hoping for?) It may seem unfair, but we're all judged partially on the company we keep. We're not suggesting that you should never ask a date to escort you to a business function, just be sure you both know "what's expected" before you do.

All right, you have a point. Dave reads Russian novels, volunteers at the animal shelter, and reads to the blind when he's not running his lucrative air freight company. But you didn't see him chew his thumbnail last Christmas, did you?

Think Like a Professional

We hope that all your dates will be charming, and that no "dating disasters" will ever happen to you, but if they do, don't give up! Keep a sense of "professionalism." You're a love recruiter and you've got a **Job** to do. It may not be easy but it will be worth it! If your date turns out to be a disaster, keep your sense of humor and write all those details in your dating log afterwards.

We reviewed our own dating logs many times in the course of writing this book, and all of the sad, ridiculous, and hilarious memories came back to us. It may be hard to believe right now, but some day you will look back and laugh. We did!

THE BOTTOM LINE

"Experience is a good school, but the fees are high."
Heinrich Heine

From the desk of: The Advice Sisters

TO: *You Company* Recruiter

FROM: Alison and Jessica

RE: Summary of Chapter 7:
Improving Your Interviewing Skills

1. Don't give out too much personal information when you first meet potential candidates.

2. Arrange your own transportation and meet in a public place. Don't leave your car and go to a second location. Get directions.

3. Safety begins at home. Don't let someone into your home until you're sure you want them there.

4. Never have sex to be accommodating. Never have unprotected sex for any reason.

5. Drinking and drugs can sabotage your search.

6. Neither you nor your date should display or accept bad dating behavior.

Summary Blueprint

From the desk of: The Advice Sisters

Today's Date: _____

1. Make sure your transportation is arranged (and functioning) before each date. Get directions.

I will complete this by: _____

2. Select some dating locales on your own turf.

I will complete this by: _____

3. Arrange for a "dating buddy" before your dates.

I will complete this by: _____

4. If you think you may have sex, be sure that you have condoms.

I will complete this by: _____

5. Avoid dating disasters by preparing for each date. Be sure to ask/inform about social activities in advance.

I will complete this by: _____

6. Go on to Chapter 8.

I will complete this by: _____

Action Memo

Okay, you ask to use the restroom, then I'll pretend to choke and beg for water.

From the desk of: The Advice Sisters

TO: *You Company* Recruiter

FROM: Alison and Jessica

RE: Chapter 8: Adjusting the *You Company* Recruiting Plan

    You've prepared yourself well for recruiting love and should be feeling truly confident about your progress. However, even the most expert love recruiters can hit an unforeseen problem or obstacle that **temporarily** slows or stalls their search.

    This chapter will help you use your experiences and your new dating tools to make necessary adjustments, and will inspire you to stay motivated, even if the road gets a little rough!

15-Second Memo

Recruiting Love is a Process

You've already put a lot of time and effort into your search and by now it should be paying off. Sometimes though, your ideal candidate accepts another "offer" or turns out to have negatives you didn't realize. Maybe you've decided that you require some qualities that weren't in your original job description. Whatever the reasons, if your search is not progressing as smoothly as you would like, you need to adjust your plan.

An executive recruiter may interview dozens of candidates before finding the right one, or s/he may decide that none of them are a match. When this happens, the recruiter reviews his/her notes, analyzes what's missing, and interviews a new group of candidates. This takes time and effort, but a good recruiter knows that it's time well spent. If the process is rushed and the wrong candidate is selected, it will ultimately be a waste of valuable time and energy. It's the same for recruiting love.

Unlike the executive recruiter, you are both the recruiter and the client. As the *You Company* employer, you must be honest with yourself about whether to revise the job description or the *You Company Profile*. As the recruiter, it is your job to adjust your strategy. The sooner you do this, the more quickly your love search can get back on track.

We understand that you would like to get the recruitment process over with quickly, so you can have a lifetime of love and happiness, but DON'T RUSH! Just like the executive recruiter who doesn't find a perfect fit among the first batch of candidates, you might also need to dig deeper to find what you really want. Remember: **making adjustments does NOT mean that you're not succeeding in your search!**

Analyze and Adjust Your Plan

A run of disappointing dates or a low response to a personal ad may make you feel anxious, but your search is probably going just fine. Each search is different, but we can tell you that yours will go more quickly if:

- Your You Company candidate job description remains accurate and you've selected applicants that closely match your requirements.
- Your You Company Profile is candid and thorough, and you're presenting yourself in a positive manner.
- You have a well-crafted dating plan and you've been doing plenty of well-targeted (as well as some general) recruiting activities.
- You're keeping your dating log faithfully.
- You are making good use of your dating tips and tools.

If you've done all these things for some time and still haven't met **any good candidates**, you may have overlooked something important.

Your *You Company Candidate Job Description* and *You Company Profile* should be superb road maps. However, you may realize that you weren't initially clear about your true needs and feelings. If you know what adjustments are necessary, make them right away! If you're still unsure about what adjustments to make:

- Plan some time and a quiet place where you can revisit some of your initial thoughts.
- Review your work from Chapters 2, 3, and 4. Are your answers still valid? If you said your primary objective is marriage, does it still hold true?

- ♥ Read your dating log carefully. Do you still like the same types of people as when you began? If so, what is the primary appeal of your candidates then and now? Are you still attracted to people who are afraid of commitment even though you swear you don't go looking for them? What qualities may be causing you to reject candidates?

- ♥ According to your dating log, are you recruiting candidates in places they will most likely be?

- ♥ Are you applying your candidate qualifications to the people you're recruiting, or are you just falling back into the familiar pattern of going out with whoever asks you?

Do These Stories Sound Familiar?

Read the following stories (all true) and ask yourself: could any of these stories have been written about me or my candidates?

Are You Sincere About What You Want, Or Are You Looking for the Right Candidate in the Wrong Places?

> ▶ Antoinette said:
> I'm Italian, and I want to marry a sophisticated, high-powered Italian man. I also love to bowl. I like it so much that I'm spending more and more of my free time at the bowling alley. They've got really good music, inexpensive beers, and a lot of hot looking hunks coming in after work from the local construction crews. I know that I probably

> won't meet too many high-powered men at the bowling alley, but you never know. Besides, the construction workers are hardworking, honest and down-to-earth. And they look terrific, too! I keep planning to join my local Italian heritage society, but right now I'm really having lots of fun, and I don't have time to do everything!

It's pretty obvious that Antoinette needs a reality check. If she really wants to meet the kind of man she says she wants, she's way off base spending all her time at the bowling lanes. Antoinette may believe that she wants to recruit a high-powered, Italian man, but from what she **says and does**, she is happy with the men she is meeting.

If Antoinette really does intend to meet sophisticated Italian men, she needs to adjust her targeting and marketing strategy. The same may be true for **you** if months have gone by without a good candidate. If you want to meet a motorcycle enthusiast, you're far less likely to find one at a horse show than at a Harley Davidson club! If you want to meet a ballerina, you will have a better chance volunteering to paint sets for the local ballet company than spending your free time at baseball games!

Can You Spot a Candidate When you See One?

Is it possible that you've recruited good candidates but you don't recognize them?

We'd never suggest that you "settle," but have you created standards in your job description that no one could meet? You might need to realistically look at your candidate qualifications if you:

Recruiting Love

- ♥ Can't seem to connect with good candidates
- ♥ Aren't sure which candidate you want to select
- ♥ Can't decide whether to move a relationship forward with one special candidate

If your special someone must be a famous sports star who is also a celebrated trumpet player, there certainly won't be many (and maybe not **any**) people who could fill that exact description. Did you really intend to describe (and could you be happy with) someone who is talented in both sports and music? If so, perhaps you'd like someone who has won many sports competitions and who also occasionally plays the trumpet in local jazz clubs. That's **still** a tall order, but more attainable.

> ▶ Bobbie said:
> I've done all of the steps to recruit love, but there is NO ONE out there who suits my needs. I'm not asking for much: just a 40-year-old man who owns his own business in something exciting — like the entertainment industry. He should look great — something like Fabio — and no one pudgy or short. Absolutely no one who wears collarless shirts or loafers. He should have a good sense of humor. However, if he laughs too loud, or likes to watch sports he's out. He's got to be physically fit — maybe work out at the gym four or five times a week — but not be obsessed with his looks. Oh, and he should be really successful so we can live in luxury and he can give me lots of expensive gifts. Naturally, my ideal candidate must be powerful and aggressive in business, but sensitive and

> always ready to be with me when I'm lonely — he must want to put my needs first. Patrick met a lot of these criteria, but he laughed like a goat and he looked like the type who might put on weight eventually. I just couldn't chance it so I stopped taking his calls. Stan owns a multi-million dollar company and also meets most of my criteria — but he is too involved in work, and is always jetting off someplace to do business. He takes me along sometimes, but I get bored amusing myself or sitting at the pool. You can see why he isn't right for me.

Incredibly, Bobbie has actually recruited two candidates that come exceedingly close to what she wants. However no ordinary mortal could satisfy Bobbie — even the slightest possibility of a weight gain is enough to push someone right off her list! And it doesn't take a rocket scientist to see that Bobbie's standards are not only impossible, they're contradictory: how can she expect a successful person to stay successful if he's spending all his time with her?

Are Others Influencing What You Really Want?

Sometimes your family and friends can give you great insight about your ideal candidate, but this can be taken to extremes! Some recruiters get thrown off the track by well-meaning friends and relatives who insist they know what's best.

> ▶ Jenna said:
> Ron and I had been dating for three years. I knew that Ron wanted to remain single, but he

Yes, it's a nice party, but it's a waste of my time. I'll never find a neurosurgeon ice hockey player with hazel eyes, over six foot two here tonight.

knew that I wanted marriage. No matter how I tried to broach the subject with him, Ron always dodged it. Ron's father was a big influence on him, and often made comments about how happy he would be if Ron and I tied the knot. When Ron got a job in another state and asked me to go with him, I insisted I wouldn't go unless we were engaged. I was ecstatic when Ron agreed. I never considered that he might have just finally given in to the pressure from both his father and me. Although I didn't know it at the time, Ron's father had threatened to stop his inheritance unless he "got some sense and settled down." Our engagement wasn't happy, and I eventually left Ron and married someone else. Ron however, is still single and happy about it.

Do You Have An Itchy Wedding Ring Finger?

If you follow the *Recruiting Love* plan, it's only a matter of time before you succeed. However, some love recruiters become so maniacal about their search that they broadcast desperation instead of interest. They can be attractive, intelligent, charming people, but they scare their candidates away.

▶ JoAnne said:
As far back as I can remember, I've dreamed about my wedding day. As a little girl, I once found an old bridal magazine and sent away for all the free information in the back. The advertisers, who didn't realize that I was 10-years old, besieged my parents with so many calls asking about 'JoAnne's

wedding date' that they starting answering the phone with: "the wedding's off!"

I've always had plenty of dates, but never a serious relationship. Not too long ago I met Jerry. He wasn't the world's most exciting man, but he said he was looking for a serious relationship. We'd been dating three long months when I mentioned that I'd like a honeymoon in Venice. Since Valentine's Day was just two months away, and we'd have been dating five whole months by then, I kept pointing out jewelry store windows and dropping hints about how Valentine's Day is the most romantic time to get engaged. Two weeks before Valentine's Day, he called to say things were moving too fast, and he wasn't ready for marriage. Why are all the men I meet afraid of commitment?

Do Your Communication Skills Need Polishing?

▶ Bertrand said:

When my wife died, everyone tried to fix me up with single women. I'd often refuse because I'm shy, but one night a friend insisted that I meet his friend, Marina, who was visiting from San Diego.

The minute I saw Marina, I knew she was special. Throughout dinner I tried to get up the courage to ask her out. I dropped what I thought were obvious hints, but she didn't pick up on them. Finally, my friend came to the rescue and blurted out: "Marina, Bertrand is trying to ask you out!"

We began dating regularly, since Marina's business often brought her to Chicago. After almost two years, Marina invited me to a family reunion. The weekend was a real success and everyone seemed to like me. Back at home, I decided that I really wanted to be with Marina. I knew she couldn't move to Chicago because of her business, so I planned to propose, and move to San Diego to be with her.

I spent several weeks building up the courage to ask her. I noticed that Marina often wasn't home, but I didn't mention it to her until the night when I said as a semi-joke: "Marina, where are you these days? You didn't run off and get married, did you?" I never expected her answer: "Well actually, Bertrand," she began, "I'm not married yet, but I did just get engaged. I wanted to ask you where our relationship was heading, but I'm old fashioned and was waiting for you to bring up the subject."

Right then I should've told Marina how I felt and fought for her while I still had the chance. Instead, I just wished her well and let her slip out of my life.

Could You Have a "Blind Spot" About Yourself?

An old saying goes: "Know thyself? If I knew myself, I'd run away!" It's hard to get past our blind spots and take an honest, critical look at ourselves.

When you were preparing your *You Company Profile,* was it hard for you to judge your goals, assets and liabilities? Maybe you need to recognize your strengths and market them better. You might have also identified some possible liabilities but aren't sure how to present them in the best light.

> Steve's story:

Steve was an accomplished writer with an adventurous spirit, but he was barely 5'2" tall. He decided to use a personal ad to jump-start his search. He never mentioned his height and he got 30 responses.

Sarah, a book editor, was his first choice. When they spoke on the phone, Steve mentioned his trim build, his jet black hair, and his hazel eyes — but he didn't mention his height.

Sarah was 5'9" and said she'd wear two red roses in her hair so Steve could identify her easily. They agreed to meet in the lobby of her office building for a "quick drink after work." At the appointed time and place, Steve spotted Sarah getting off the elevator. "I'm Steve, are you Sarah?" he asked. She glanced at him quickly and then looked away. "No," she said, then walked out of the building.

Steve couldn't believe what had happened. He knew that the woman he'd just spoken to was Sarah. She had taken just one look at him and couldn't even bring herself to even have one drink with him.

As cruel as Sarah's rejection was, Steve realized he'd have to be honest about his height. If the women he met couldn't be comfortable with his size, he couldn't be comfortable with them.

From then on, Steve told candidates all about himself, including that he was only 5'2". Some said "no thanks," but some didn't care at all, and were delighted to meet him. Now he's happily married with three kids.

Are You Confusing Love and Need?

Sometimes, recruitment searches stall because the recruiter confuses love with need. In Chapter 5 you met Gus, who wanted to take his candidate to the kiddie park on their first date. He may say he wants a love of his own, but he really needs a stepmother for Bobby. If a love relationship isn't a priority for him, he'd be better off hiring a nanny, or encouraging close relationships between his son and the women he already knows.

Earlier in this chapter you met JoAnne, with the "itchy ring finger." Her primary goal should be finding a candidate she loves, but her strong need to get married overshadows everything. Eventually, JoAnne may find someone willing to marry her, but if she accepts just "anyone who asks," both of them will likely end up miserable. Consider the following statements:

- ♥ I need a mom/dad for my kids.
- ♥ I want a baby but don't want to be a single parent.
- ♥ I'm tired of explaining to people why I'm still single.
- ♥ If I live with someone else I won't need a maid, cook, mechanic, etc.
- ♥ If I find a mate, no one will think I'm gay/ambivalent.
- ♥ If I find a mate I will never be lonely again.
- ♥ My mother would stop nagging me to get married.
- ♥ If I was married I wouldn't have to worry so much about my looks, status, career, etc.
- ♥ I need a safe and monogamous sex life.
- ♥ I'd have a better standard of living if I got married.

If any of those statements apply to you, you must decide if you really want a love relationship, or if you're looking for something else that you feel a relationship can give you. "Selling one's soul" is a matter of conscience, but before you act out of pure **need** rather than love, **we urge you** to consider that there's usually another way to fulfill that need without involving someone in a relationship.

> ▶ Cynthia's story:
> Cynthia is in her early forties and she desperately wants a baby. The trouble is, she's attracted to well-established and much older men who already have grown children and don't want to start a second family. She dates these men because she craves the status, power, money and attention that older men lavish on her. However, she is acutely aware that her biological clock is ticking and that if she doesn't actively start recruiting someone who wants to start a family, she'll lose that option. Meanwhile, she is unable to choose between her need for money and status and her need to have a family. In any case, love has little to do with her choices.

Could You be Sabotaging Your Efforts?

If you've done all the steps to recruit love and the search still hasn't produced a candidate, you might be sabotaging your search with poor dating behavior! In Chapter 7, we showed you ways in which people unknowingly sabotage their search. Even if you think you're a "great catch," someone else will think you're a "toad" if you are socially inept, rude, or a poor sport.

▶ Simon's story:
Simon wasn't what you'd call a "hunk," but he was a nice guy with a heart of gold. He really wanted to get married and start a family, but although he dated a lot of women, few accepted a second date with him.

We couldn't figure out what Simon's problem was, until we double-dated with him. Simon showed up for his date not in his usual well-cut business suit, but in a loud, tight, silk shirt, unbuttoned nearly to his waist. He had a huge chain around his neck with a large gold dog tag on it "for conversation." He flirted openly and suggestively with the waitress, told off-color jokes, and dropped names of politicians he "knew." Worse, Simon didn't stop pawing his date all through dinner, even though it made her, and the rest of us, squirm. This wasn't the polite, thoughtful Simon we knew. Dr. Jekyll had turned into Mr. Hyde!

Later, we told Simon he was sabotaging his dates, and he admitted that he altered "how he really was" because he didn't think he was "interesting enough." Once we set Simon straight, he quickly found the woman of his dreams. Simon and his wife have now been married nine years, are the parents of five beautiful children and they are still very much in love!

Are You and Your Candidate Really Ready For A Committed Relationship?

Sometimes, men and women who insist there's no one "out there" for them actually aren't ready for a serious partnership. Could you be like Henry or Rachel?

▶ Henry's story:

Henry is handsome and writes poetry, but he rarely dates. Unopened boxes still line the walls of the apartment he moved into almost a year ago, and his refrigerator holds only a six pack of beer and some stale cheese. Henry would like to try out reciting some of his work before a live audience — but so far, he hasn't. Most evenings Henry frequents the Pussycat Club. He likes the waitress, Amber, and thinks a lot about asking her out — but he never does. He tells his friend, Pete, how lucky he is to be married to Alice, but he can't imagine ever settling for someone like her because she's no "spring chicken" and Henry is only attracted to "girls" who look like models.

Henry insists he wants to get married and keeps telling himself that he'll know when the right woman comes along. His dating log lists all the women he's met with all their flaws: too old, too dumpy, too intellectual, too dumb, etc. As he approaches his fifty-seventh birthday he's still thinking about "being a dad" — when he meets the woman of his dreams.

▶ Rachel's story:

Rachel looks younger than her real age, since she diets and exercises regularly. She was proposed to at the age of twenty-two, but she wasn't ready to "settle down right then." She's never received another offer of marriage, but "there's still time," she says. Rachel also complains that she can't find anyone special — but she's scheduled her free time so there isn't a minute left for

> dating: exercise, laundry, yoga class etc. — every night of the week. Last year, a man did ask her out, but for the night of the season finale of her favorite television show. She turned him down and told him why. He never asked her out again.

Francine looks like an excellent candidate, but her appeal wears thin as people discover that she's really not ready for a serious relationship.

> ▶ John said:
> When I met Francine through a video dating service I thought I'd hit the jackpot. She was incredibly pretty, intelligent, and lots of fun. She always said the "right things," and made me feel special. But the closer I got, the more distant Francine became. She blew hot — then cold. I started dating other women, but when I backed off, Francine warmed up again! It took me a while to realize there was a pattern: whenever I retreated Francine would pursue me — when I responded, she'd back off again!
> Eventually, I stopped calling Francine altogether. Soon I met a terrific woman, and wouldn't you know it — when Francine saw our engagement announcement in the paper she called to say she missed me and asked me if I'd like to go out with her again!

Are You Confusing Sex and Love?

"Chemistry" is definitely an important part of any intimate relationship, but it's not enough to sustain a long-term commitment. Sometimes, your physical attraction to a candidate can get in the way of your true assessment. Your feelings may be nothing more than pure sexual desire if you find that:

- ♥ You are more interested in having sex with your candidate than in doing anything else.
- ♥ You don't have much in common.
- ♥ You struggle to have meaningful conversation.
- ♥ You are so physically attracted that you can't rationally assess the candidate's ultimate potential.

> Jacob said:
> From the moment I saw Danielle I felt incredible lust for her. She apparently felt the same way too, because despite the fact that we both knew it was a terrible idea, we had sex on our first date — and it was incredible! Danielle was attractive and adventurous, and I felt really lucky to be with her. I was sure that I was in love with Danielle, but I soon realized that we had absolutely nothing in common except that we had fun in bed, which is where we spent most of our time together.

Is it Too Early For You to Recruit Love Again?

How do you know when you, or a candidate you're considering, is ready to love again? Everyone needs time to regroup from a disappointment or a loss, and it's not a good idea to start over immediately.

If either you or your candidate has been widowed or divorced (especially after a long marriage) or if either of you have just ended a serious relationship, be careful.

Either you or your candidate may think you're ready for a relationship, but perhaps all you can handle now is a warm friendship. Do any of the following apply?

- ♥ You've recently had a loss and you keep getting cold feet with good candidates.
- ♥ You selected a new candidate who, coincidentally, could be a double for your former love.
- ♥ Your new love has the same negative traits of your former love that caused your breakup in the first place.
- ♥ Your new love is the exact opposite of your former love.

If you've recently come out of a long-term relationship (by choice or not) you may feel that no one can ever replace what you've lost. However, even people who were in long relationships eventually crave companionship, and some of their new relationships blossom into love — even marriage. You don't have to recreate the relationship you had before to find love now.

In Chapter 7 you met Sandra, who realized on her first date with Gary that he wasn't ready to be "back in circulation" when he blubbered about his ex-girlfriend. When the time is right, Gary will make a good candidate for someone, but now, he's just a liability.

If you feel "gun shy" from a painful relationship, remember the good news! Statistics show that the majority of people who have been married once will marry again, usually within the first few years after their divorce. The second time around is usually a lot better.

> Diana said:
> On our wedding day I kept thinking: Fred's so wonderful, and I'm so lucky! But we began fighting the minute we returned from our honeymoon. Fred demanded that I only serve the foods he liked and see the friends he approved of. He insisted on picking out my clothes and hairstyle even when they didn't suit me. He cheated on me three months after our wedding, then said it was justified because I wasn't a good wife. I should've left then. Fred continued a steady pattern of cheating and blaming me. One night after a particularly ugly fight, I threw him out and started divorce proceedings the next day.
>
> The divorce was long and difficult. Only my job kept me going. It was obvious that Richard, one of the assistant managers, liked me, but I was in so much pain that I never even considered that he might be a good candidate. We were friends, but I wasn't ready to date. One night Richard, and another woman from the store made plans to go to the movies. The other woman canceled at the last minute, so Richard and I went together. We had a great time. It took me many more months to finally get over the divorce, but Richard never pushed for more of a commitment than I was ready to make. When we finally did decide to get married, I knew that it would last.

If you can't seem to bounce back even after some time has passed, it's time to get outside professional help. The sooner you do, the sooner you can keep going. You can help your own healing process by doing all or some of the following:

- Divert your attention from the breakup and focus on avoiding the same situation in future relationships.
- Spend your time with friends doing things you enjoy.
- Occupy your mind with other facets of your life for a little while.
- Remember that recruiting love is an adventure, and be sure to try new things when you're ready to date again.
- Tell yourself that your last relationship was only a "dress rehearsal" for the real thing.
- Thumb through your dating log to see if there's anyone you enjoyed dating but "gave up on" so that you could be with your last special love. Why not call and see if those other potential candidates are still free? Most former candidates will be flattered that you remembered them, whether or not they're interested in dating you again. By the way, in case you think this never works, read this!

> Yvonne said:
> I was heartbroken when Bruce broke up with me but eventually, I took out my dating log and looked over the contacts from the personal ad I'd placed six months before. Sandwiched between my early dates with Bruce was something I'd written about Ted. I had enjoyed my two dates with him, so I called. To my surprise, Ted was delighted to hear from me! He asked me out for dinner the following day, and the rest is history. Within five months we were engaged, and within a year we were married! This time I've packed my dating log away for good!

Are You Unable to Tell Mr. or Ms. Toad to Hit The Road?

There is an law of physics that also applies to your love search: *"Two objects cannot occupy the same space at the same time."* It's impossible to search for someone new if you old love is still in the picture.

> Andrew said:
> I'd been dating Tamara for five years — seven, if you count the numerous, stormy breakups. I knew that she was wrong for me — she cheated constantly, didn't feel comfortable with my family and friends, and had no ambition about the future. Nevertheless, I was attracted to her because she was attractive, wild and exciting. I think she liked me because I gave her the security that she never had before. When I began recruiting love, I thought I'd have the willpower to break up with Tamara for good when Ms. Right came along. But I never let a relationship develop with anyone else because Tamara was front and center in my mind! Inevitably, we'd fight and break up for the same reasons all over again. Finally, I had to accept that I would never be free to find someone else if I didn't get Tamara out of my life for good.

Using Your Dating Log to Get Back on Track

If you've been faithfully recording information in your dating log, you'll probably see some patterns by now. Do you see any signs that perhaps you, and not your candidates, might be the primary cause of any problems? Even though you're the recruiter, your candidates will also be judging you. It's easy to complain that there are no good candidates and scrutinize everyone's drawbacks but your own. It takes insight, intelligence, and courage to realize that you might also be making some mistakes. And it takes a lot of courage to fix them.

Review your dating log closely and read between the lines. Now is the time to adjust your strategy so that you can get back on the right track.

Keep Moving Forward!

Even if you haven't yet been as successful as you'd like, keep moving toward your goal. If you are enjoying your recruiting activities, continue to do them!

> Maria said:
> I love making things grow and being outdoors, so I volunteered at a local community garden. I seemed to have a lot in common with Martin, who had just begun to plant the vegetable patch next to mine. We agreed to meet for dinner. I hoped that he'd be "the one" for me, but that evening, Martin barely acknowledged me. He hadn't bothered to shave, and he was wearing his dirty gardening clothes. He'd talked a blue streak when we met, but now it was a struggle to get a word out of him. As we waited for the check after an endless meal, Martin lowered the boom: "Maria, I like you, but to be honest, I'm not attracted to you. Also, I've just met someone else. I was going to cancel our date but I lost your phone number, and I didn't want to stand you up. We can still be friends, okay?"

> I was shocked. I drove home, angry at myself for thinking Martin had potential as a special candidate. I considered quitting, but I kept gardening because I really enjoy it. A few months later I met William, and he asked me out. I wasn't sure I was ready to date anyone else from the garden, but I decided to take a chance.
>
> That was nine months ago. Tomorrow we're picking up our wedding rings!

Do You Need to Take a Break?

Recruiting Love should be challenging, but it should **never** become a dreaded chore! If it does, you need to take a break. But first, review your assessments and your dating log while they're still fresh in your mind. A few weeks without active recruiting probably won't hurt your momentum, and afterwards, you'll feel refreshed and ready to get back into action. Don't shut yourself in! You can be social without actively recruiting. Spend time with your family and friends. Go on vacation. Continue doing the activities you enjoy (like Maria, the community gardener). You might just find someone when you're not really looking. For now, just put the thought of actively recruiting out of your mind. When you finally decide to resume, you'll feel re-energized and will conduct a better search.

If you step out of circulation too long, you may lose many of the contacts you've made. If you need a break from interviewing, but you're dating possible candidates that you don't want to lose, tell them you're going to be very busy at work for the next few weeks and probably won't be able to see them for a little while. Leave "thinking of you" messages on their answering machines during the day when they won't be home to answer the phone. They'll think you're buried in work and will be flattered that you took the time to call! Some may not wait, but most will be glad to see you again; and you'll see them with a new, fresh, perspective.

You can also take a break without losing momentum by changing the types of activities that you've been doing. If you've been participating heavily in group activities and singles functions, consider placing a personal ad. Stay home and let the candidates come to you. When you're ready for more active meeting, recruiting, and dating, you'll have a new bunch of possible candidates to consider! If you find you've been relying on solitary activities such as the matchmakers, the Internet, and personal ads, consider trying out a singles club to see what it's like to be with a lot of singles all at once!

Find Support In a Dating Success Team

We hope that recruiting love has been a positive experience for you so far — but if you'd like strength and inspiration from others who are going through the same thing, you might consider joining a **dating success team**, or starting one of your own. Members of a success team meet regularly and share their experiences, but unlike group therapy or career counseling, success teams focus on **action** and **results**. Success teams are more traditionally used by job hunters, but they can also inspire and empower you in your search for love.

> Walter said:
> I'm divorced and have custody of my two kids, so when I was ready to look for love again I needed some impartial advice and support to get started.

> I saw an ad for a dating success team and was pretty nervous about calling, but the woman was so nice that I forgot to stay nervous. Patty was a non-profit manager who was also a single parent. She invited me to the first meeting of the dating support group she was forming.
>
> Two nights later, at a local coffee shop, six of us agreed to a two-hour meeting each week. Our group was pretty diverse: a financial analyst, a computer programmer, a secretary, a lawyer, a non-profit manager and a construction worker, ranging in age from 30 to 55. Our differences made for some eye-opening discussions.
>
> After we got to know each other, we took turns hosting the meetings in our homes. We spent some time griping, but we mostly tried to support and motivate each other. If I told the group I was going to compose a personal ad, I'd think twice before not doing it because I'd have to report on my progress at the next session. Their feedback about my ad really helped me, too.
>
> As time went on we became good friends. Some of the initial members dropped out, but others took their places, so the group remained lively and strong. Several times, group members offered to baby sit for my kids so I could go out. I actually met my wife through a friend of one of the group members. Without a doubt, the dating support team made recruiting love easier!

Starting Your Own Dating Success Team

If you can't find any dating success teams in your area, try starting one of your own. Just place an ad in the "personals" section of your local paper. Until everyone gets to know each other, hold the meetings in a local restaurant. Later on, you can take turns hosting.

Whether you join an established team or start a new one, remember that support teams are active sessions where everyone both **listens & participates.** One member of the group is designated as the time keeper and group leader for that session. Each member gets equal time to report on his or her progress and to ask for help. This assistance usually takes the form of:

- ♥ **Brainstorming,** or asking the group for as many ideas as possible pertaining to a specific need or problem;

- ♥ **Barn Raising,** or asking the group to help solve a problem or to help obtain needed information;

- ♥ **Role Playing,** using the group as a test audience to rehearse a verbal presentation, provide feedback on written materials, or walk through a particular problem or situation;

- ♥ **Sympathy,** asking the group to help relieve stress and be a sympathetic "ear."

The important thing is for group members to commit themselves to participate and attend regularly. Members who continually miss sessions should be asked to leave the group.

Make Your Dreams Real: Do a Self-Affirmation

Sometimes, the best thing you can do to help speed your search is to simply **keep telling yourself** that you're going to succeed. We like self-affirmations: reminding yourself in a tangible way that you **can** and **will** meet your special someone. Get a package of sticky notes and write something positive on each, such as: "I'm desirable," or "I'm going to meet my special someone any day now." Put them on your bathroom mirror, your refrigerator — anywhere you're likely to see them. Every time you see these messages you'll reinforce your positive feelings about your love search. Repeat the messages to yourself while you're driving to work, on line at the market, in the shower, etc. Your message can be anything you choose, but the more often you see it and say it, the faster you'll achieve it.

> Hannah said:
> To be honest, I thought self-affirmations were dumb, but I was willing to try anything. I put little messages everywhere — even on the dashboard of my car! I started feeling more upbeat and optimistic, and before long, I noticed that I was attracting more positive attention from men.
>
> Four weeks later, I had to fly out of town on a business trip. On the flight, the man sitting next to me asked me if I'd like to share some wine. I discovered that Ben sold the type of novelty items my advertising agency needed. When I got back to my office, I found a dozen pink roses on my desk with a card from Ben asking me to dinner. At first, I thought he just wanted to get my company's business, but he kept calling even after they selected another vendor. We've been dating over a year now, and things are still going really well!

Some Important Words To Consider

No matter how excellent you are as a love recruiter, you may occasionally come home disappointed from an endless evening. However, if you follow the *Recruiting Love* plan, you will kiss a lot **fewer** toads, and you'll have far less dating horror stories to your credit.

When you first wrote your *You Company* candidate job description in Chapter 2, you established a target date for finalizing your search. Go back now and re-evaluate your time frame.

- ♥ Does it still seem viable?
- ♥ Did it allow enough time for adjustments to your plan?

If not, you must go back and adjust your target date. In business, you will often have to make adjustments to a project plan, even if it causes a delay.

If you're worried that your search won't ever produce results, **RELAX!** There is absolutely **NO NEED TO PANIC**. You didn't do all that research and data collection for nothing. Be encouraged! If you've found a problem, you're now going to fix it. You are a love recruiter — not a helpless victim of circumstances! You are in **control**!

We'll say it one more time to make sure you engrave it in your mind: Making adjustments to your plan is NOT a setback, it's a sign that you are getting closer!

=========== The Bottom Line ===========

"When one has made a mistake, one says: 'Next time I shall really know what to do.' What one should say is: 'I already know what I shall really do next time.'"
Ceasare Pavese

From the desk of: The Advice Sisters

TO: *You Company* Recruiter

FROM: Alison and Jessica

RE: Summary of Chapter 8: Adjusting the *You Company* Recruiting Plan

Summary Blueprint

1. It takes careful assessment, planning, reassessment and adjustment to make a love search successful — and you can't rush through this.

2. The *Recruiting Love* plan will make this process easier and faster; however, failing to identify and remove obstacles can delay your success.

3. The most important TOOLS to help you reassess how your plan is going are:

    ♥ Your You Company Candidate Job Description and your You Company Profile

    ♥ Your dating log

    ♥ A willingness to adjust your own behavior

4. The most common problems that can stall your search (but you *can* fix them) are:

    ♥ You still don't know what kind of person you really want.

    ♥ You're not being honest with yourself about your real needs.

From the desk of: The Advice Sisters

- ♥ You're looking for the right person in the wrong places.
- ♥ No ordinary mortal could meet your candidate qualifications.
- ♥ Your communication skills could use some work.
- ♥ You're unable to spot a good candidate when you see one.
- ♥ You've got a "blind spot" about yourself or your candidate.
- ♥ You have an "itchy ring finger."
- ♥ You (or your candidate) are not ready for the committed relationship you say you want.
- ♥ You are confusing love with other needs.
- ♥ Your physical attraction to your candidate is clouding the overall picture.
- ♥ You need a break from recruiting love.
- ♥ You are still on the rebound and it's too early for another love.
- ♥ Mr. or Ms. Wrong is taking all your energies.
- ♥ You unknowingly sabotage your dates with inappropriate behavior.

Summary Blueprint

From the desk of: The Advice Sisters

5. Some TIPS to deal with delays:
   - ♥ Spend time with friends.
   - ♥ Keep your mind occupied with something other than dating.
   - ♥ Use your dating log to restart your search.
   - ♥ Do self-affirmations.
   - ♥ If you've found a problem, be encouraged that you are going to fix it.
   - ♥ Remind yourself that reassessments are NOT setbacks!

6. Some TIPS to deal with burnout:
   - ♥ Take time off if you need it.
   - ♥ Join, or start a dating success team.
   - ♥ Focus on activities you enjoy — not just those that you use to recruit love.
   - ♥ Try a recruiting method that you haven't done yet.
   - ♥ Keep believing in yourself and in *Recruiting Love* and soon you will have the love you want.

From the desk of: The Advice Sisters

Today's Date: _____

    1. If you've hit a setback, review this chapter carefully. Use your dating log, your *You Company Candidate Job Description* and your *You Company Profile* to analyze problems and adjust your recruiting plan.

I will complete this by: _____

    2. Plan to take some time off if you need a break.

I will complete this by: _____

    3. Get a package of sticky notes, and write positive messages on them. Put them wherever you'll be most likely to see them.

I will complete this by: _____

Action Memo

From the desk of: The Advice Sisters

Action Memo

4. If you want to, join a dating success team or start one of your own.

I will complete this by: _____

5. If you need to, reread the tips for reassessment and burnout, and try a few of them.

I will complete this by: _____

6. Encourage yourself to get back on track. Remind yourself that reassessment and readjustment are just part of the process, and it doesn't mean you're failing!

I will complete this by: _____

7. Go on to Chapter 9.

I will complete this by: _____

From the desk of: The Advice Sisters

TO: *You Company* Recruiter

FROM: Alison and Jessica

RE: Chapter 9: Selecting The Final Candidate (Making an Offer)

By now, you've probably interviewed a lot of candidates. If you have found one exceptional candidate, or several excellent finalists, it's time to:

♥ Make an offer to the exceptional candidate, or:

♥ Select one of the finalists and make an offer.

If no one has stood out in this search, or you've made an offer that has been refused, you will now need to re-evaluate your plan and start again. In this chapter, we will help you make some decisions and resolve dilemmas you may have about the candidates and the search process.

15-Second Memo

At some point in every job search, an executive recruiter reviews the information about the top contenders, selects one ideal candidate or narrows the finalists to a select few, and makes a recommendation to the client. The client then considers the pros and cons of each candidate, offers the job to the one that most closely matches the requirements. Several excellent candidates may be considered, but only one will get the position.

Perhaps you were a finalist for a position for which you met all of the requirements, but you didn't get the job. You may have known in your heart that you were almost perfect — but someone matched the employer's requirements even more closely. In your love search, there may be just one candidate, or several potentially excellent candidates. All may be almost perfect, but there will be one candidate that most closely matches your requirements. *This* time, you get to make the choice! It would be easy if you could just look at the pros and cons of each candidate on paper and mathematically choose the one with the highest score, but love searches don't work exactly that way!

How Do I Know When It's Right?

In a love search, the decision-making process is only absolutely smooth and perfect on paper. Although we have stressed the importance of research and planning, your final decision about whether to select one special candidate — or none at all, will still depend on what your heart tells you, as well as your mind.

For centuries, men and women have been wondering: "How will I know if it's right?" Your mother probably told you, "You'll just know in your heart when you've found the right one." Your final decision will be made, in part, as it has been for centuries — with your heart and your "gut." **However**, you'll get tremendous help from the careful planning you've done all along! If you've stuck with the plan this long, you can rest assured that you're not relying on chance.

If you recruited love using the plan in this book, you took the time to assess yourself and your requirements. Therefore, when you find and recruit an outstanding candidate, you will know it in you heart and your mind AND you will also have solid facts to back you up! At some point, if a superior candidate hasn't come along, you will also know when to abandon this particular search and start fresh.

How Do I Know If I Want to Make an Offer?

On your *You Company Candidate Job Description,* you specified a target date for completing the search. However, there is no exact or proper time to make an offer to a candidate, or begin a new search. We know a man who met a superior candidate and made her an offer within a week — and she accepted! We also know a couple who dated for eight years before they married. For each candidate that you are seriously considering, check off those items which apply to you.

❏ This person meets all or most of your requirements for the ideal candidate.

❏ You have discussed the possibilities of a future together including marriage and children.

❏ You have dated this candidate for at least six months consistently (if not exclusively) at least once a week.

- ☐ You are not interested in pursuing a relationship with anyone else because your instincts tell you that this candidate is "the one" for you.

- ☐ You feel comfortable with your candidate, even if you're not "doing anything special."

- ☐ You feel that you and your candidate have a complete "relationship" and are not just "dating."

- ☐ If your candidate has children, you have met them and spent time with them.

- ☐ There is real chemistry (physical, emotional and intellectual attraction) between you.

- ☐ You have met most of your candidate's close friends and probably some of his/her co-workers.

- ☐ You have met his family, and have been invited to family events and holiday celebrations (especially if they live nearby).

- ☐ Even if you aren't living together, you have exchanged keys and/or have some of your belongings at your candidate's apartment and vice versa.

- ☐ You've taken a vacation together and it "went well."

If you've checked all or most of the statements for a specific candidate, chances are your relationship is at a decision point.

What to Consider Before Making an Offer

If you've followed the steps in *Recruiting Love* and have used your new dating tools, you should have little or no trouble deciding when, and to whom, to extend an offer. However people rarely appear in perfect packages. If you have one or more final candidates, ask yourself:

- ♥ How much adjustment will be required to make it work with this candidate—considering the whole package?
- ♥ Are there any "must have" requirements that my candidate doesn't have? What, if anything, compensates for that?
- ♥ Does my candidate have any of the traits (even in small amounts) that I had said are unacceptable?

If, on the whole, your answers indicate you're happy with the direction your relationship is heading, and you're satisfied with the overall qualifications of your candidate, you're probably ready to make an offer.

If You're Still Unsure

Sometimes even after examining all the facts, you may not be certain. Relax! We understand that picking a special love is a bigger commitment than picking a job. Using your *You Company* candidate assessment, job description, and your dating log, ask yourself:

- Which, if any, of my requirements have changed since I began my search?

- Has my ideal candidate changed since we first met, either for the better, or not? How has s/he changed and what caused it?

- Qualifications aside, how do I really feel about this candidate deep down — not just off the top of my head? Does being with this person really enhance my life — or am I just tired of recruiting?

- How satisfied am I with my candidate on the whole? If I'm not satisfied, is it because I'm temporarily bored, upset, or unsure about other things in my life? Am I simply envious of my friends and their partners? (If only she was sexier like Carla — if only we could afford a nicer house like Ned and Nina.) Many good relationships have been ended, to massive regret later on, because the recruiter thought that the "grass would be greener" elsewhere!

- Are external forces (pressures at work, meddling family and friends) pushing us together or pulling us apart?

- Is another love interest clouding the situation?

- Am I trying to force this relationship to work?

- Have I stopped trying to make this relationship work?

- Do we want very different lifestyles? (You want to live in the city — his dream is to own a farm; he wants at least three children and you don't even want pets; you want to live in a big house and he thinks you should both join the Peace Corps.)

- Do we have clashing religious beliefs or moral values?

- Are we always fighting over the same things? Are we absolutely unable to compromise?
- Do we have a problem sharing our thoughts and feelings? Do we show a lack of respect for each other's point of view when we differ?

A "Yes" to one or more of these questions may indicate a problem that you need to resolve before making an offer. If they can't be resolved, perhaps this candidate, no matter how attractive, isn't right for you.

If you've found an ideal candidate, but you're still wavering on a final offer, perhaps your own fear of commitment is the obstacle. Go back to Chapter 3 and look at your responses for the *You Company Profile*. What was your relationship goal? Has it changed? If you were unsure or ambivalent about your relationship goals when you began, you may still be confused about your real feelings. Perhaps all of your (or your candidate's) fault-finding or withdrawn behavior is occurring because your relationship has become too intimate for your comfort level! Even though you **say** that you want a committed relationship, and even though you have been successful in recruiting one, you may feel unsure about taking that last step now that you've actually found "the one."

You may also be afraid because you haven't had good role models for love. People who grew up in homes where their parents were divorced, or who had unhappy and/or abusive relationships, may understandably be fearful of getting hurt. They may be wary of accepting love and afraid that they won't be able to sustain a monogamous relationship.

If you've been single for a long time, you may worry about relinquishing some of your "independence." When you share your life with someone, you may not be able to blast your stereo while eating your TV dinner on the couch. (At least not very often, we hope!) But trust us; if you've chosen well, you'll be gaining far more than you're giving up!

I'm Worried that I'll Make an Offer and Then I'll Find Someone Better!

We've all read in novels about the bride who falls in love with her groom's best friend at the reception, or the man who realizes that he's in love with someone else as his bride is walking down the aisle. This is mainly the stuff of fiction. *Recruiting Love* is a book for adults, and we have assumed all along that you have an idea of what you want and who you want. At this point, if you've recruited enough candidates and you know in your heart that you're ready to make a decision, you should do so. You've gathered a lot of information, and compared your candidates carefully. By the time you're ready to make a choice, you should have enough confidence in yourself to know that the person you've selected is the right one.

It's natural to have at least some minor indecision about the person you select — no one is 100% perfect. However, if your choice is sound, your anxiety will pass. We hope this won't happen to you (it usually doesn't) but if after you've made a choice you still feel that the "grass is greener" elsewhere, you should immediately re-read this chapter and review your dating log to see if you made a wise decision.

Anyone Who Does THAT Can't Be Ideal!

You should never expect a person to "change" for you, but they can, and often do! No one is perfect all the time and in all situations. Even a great candidate may occasionally disappoint, hurt or anger you. No matter what was said or done, it's not wise to make or retract an offer in a fit of anger. When you are angry, disappointed or hurt, you can not consider the consequences, or even your own true feelings, carefully or objectively.

Our grandmother used to say: "Once you spit you can't pick it up." When you're upset, you may say something in anger that you will later regret. If you've had a major disagreement with an otherwise good candidate, consider the following before you make any permanent decisions:

- ♥ Is what provoked me an isolated incident or part of a pattern? If it's an isolated incident, it's not worth ending the relationship!

- ♥ What was my part in this? Did I escalate or intensify the situation?

- ♥ Even if my partner's action was inexcusable, have I given him/her an opportunity to repair it? If you haven't given your partner a chance to communicate or change, you're giving the relationship short shrift!

- ♥ Am I being so inflexible or critical that no one could meet my standards? No one is perfect, but only you can tell if your partner was totally out of line.

- ♥ Am I so angry that I'm not thinking clearly — and if I end the relationship now, will I regret it later? (We recommend a "cooling-off" period here. Take yourself to lunch or a movie, go jogging, or "sleep on it".)

Not all relationships can or should be saved. But sometimes, relationships ultimately become stronger after a serious problem is resolved.

My Candidate is Reluctant to Accept My Offer

In business, a tenacious recruiter will make the most compelling argument possible to convince an ambivalent candidate to take the job. At some point, if the candidate is clearly not interested, the recruiter must go on and consider someone else. In love recruiting, it's no different. If you and your candidate can't come to terms, at some point, you just have to move on. We know it's frustrating when you've recruited a great candidate but s/he isn't sure about making a commitment. If you know that your candidate genuinely cares for you, but is afraid to commit, it's worth discussing it, and persevering a while longer. If you're especially committed to this person, you might suggest couples counseling.

Perhaps your candidate is involved with other people and doesn't want to give them up. Maybe your own behavior is making him/her unsure about accepting your offer. If so, let the person know that you are sincerely willing to make some changes. (If we're talking about a grand transformation, that might signal that this person isn't right after all!) Spend time around friends who are happily married so that your candidate can experience what a happy marriage "feels like." Develop a hobby that's new for both of you that you can share (ballroom dancing, a book club, fitness program).

If your candidate is reluctant because of obligations (education, getting a job, switching careers, etc.) did you know about these obligations before, or might your candidate simply be stalling? Do you both agree on what "in the future" means? Are there any considerations (like your biological clock) that make you unwilling to wait very long — even for this special candidate? How long are you willing to wait before you begin a new search? No matter what the reasons, no one should ever make you feel insecure or ridiculous for wanting a committed relationship!

Should I Agree to Live Together to Get a Further Commitment?

In some cases, your chosen candidate is willing to move the relationship forward — but not to the level that you were originally looking for. We don't think that you should settle for anything less than what you want. If you want marriage, but decide to just live together because that is as far as s/he is willing to go, remember that living together often doesn't move a candidate towards marriage. (Ever hear the expression, "Why buy the cow when the milk is free?") If you decide on a trial arrangement, put a time limit on it and maintain your own apartment or house so you have a place to return to if necessary.

Be careful about pressuring your candidate into giving you what you want! Moving in together or making communal purchases before you have a wedding date is one way to get your candidate to "invest" in the relationship, but it is not a savvy decision personally or financially.

If after "negotiating" with your candidate, you cannot come to an agreement, you will have to decide whether or not to start recruiting others. Sometimes, issuing an ultimatum works, but don't bluff or do it in anger. Deliver the ultimatum in person with a clear deadline, and be prepared to follow through on it!

My Candidate Is No Longer Under Consideration How Do I Let Him/Her Know?

Even by mutual agreement, it's difficult to end a relationship with someone you have been with for a long time. However, once you are certain that you want to, or need to end your relationship with a candidate, don't drag it out. Set a target date and write it here:

I plan to end my relationship with: _____
(candidate's name)

by: _____
(your deadline)

Here are some "Do's and Don'ts" to consider when ending a long-term relationship:

- ♥ Be authoritative. Don't let a candidate think that s/he is still under consideration when you know it's over.

- ♥ Tell your candidate face-to-face and let him/her know the reasons for your final decision.

- ♥ After the breakup, it's best not to continue regular contact with the candidate, especially if s/he is holding out any hope that you may change your mind.

- ♥ Make it clear if you plan to recruit others. Under no circumstances should you accept sexual favors from a former candidate, even if s/he is willing.

- If you have been living together, suggest some viable temporary living arrangements until the two of you figure out how to proceed.
- If there are children involved, be friendly, or at least civil, for their sake.

My Candidate Turned the Job Down

In the business world, if you are a recruiter and your chosen candidate turns the job down, you don't take it as a personal rejection. You continue searching until you find another excellent candidate who does accept. As a love recruiter, it will be more difficult for you to just move on if your candidate says "no thanks." It's disappointing when you think you've recruited the perfect candidate and it doesn't work out, but look at it as a learning experience. If this happens to you (and we hope it won't) review your dating log. Were there any clues that you didn't see before? By carefully reviewing your notes (after you've cooled off!) you'll ensure you won't get turned down again!

I've Decided To Find Someone New What Should I Consider First?

If your relationship is more advanced than just occasional dating, there will be more factors to consider before you reject this candidate and recruit another one. There may also business considerations if you either work, or run a business together. There may also be financial and legal considerations. Friends and family of both parties will impact your decision, too. Some questions include:

- ♥ What is my plan for being on my own again? Will I seek another relationship or will I stay single for awhile? Am I certain I won't change my mind about the breakup?

- ♥ How will terminating the relationship affect my work, my self-esteem, my finances, my lifestyle, and my outlook?

- ♥ Would I be better off ending this relationship, or should I try harder to make it work?

- ♥ If we've been living together, who will move out? What financial/psychological effect will this have on me (and my children?)

- ♥ If we have a business or property together, do we have an acceptable plan for its disposition? Could we separate and still share property or work together?

- ♥ How will I explain my decision? How will it impact my children, friends and family?

What About Legal Concerns?

Recruiting Love is not a legal guide, so we aren't going to try to anticipate all the considerations you may face in terminating a relationship, but if you have a formal arrangement (marriage, prenuptial agreement, business partnership etc.) you probably have legal concerns.

If you are married or have children together, you must consider alimony and/or child support (NOT only awarded only to women anymore!) custody arrangements, lawyers, court fees and costs, dissolution of joint financial obligations and separate insurance, just to name a few.

Married or not, if you had a prenuptial agreement or any other type of live-in or business agreement, the terms of those contracts will likely affect the outcome. These contracts are not always set in stone, and you may need an attorney to advise you of your rights and obligations. We know of few couples who have successfully navigated the legal system on their own. However, an attorney can negotiate on your behalf, sparing you a lot of face-to-face confrontations with your "ex." Retaining an attorney can be expensive, but many will give you an initial consultation for a reasonable, set fee. Ask around, or call the local bar association for a referral.

If tempers are not high, you can save money and hassle with **arbitration**, where a mediator guides you through the legal process without protracted court proceedings.

What About Our Shared Friends and Family?

When a couple breaks up, their primary concern should be losing a partner, not about losing the partner's family and friends. In most cases, when we become part of a couple, our partner's family and friends welcome us into their circle. They may like us for who we intrinsically are, but face it, even if you're a business powerhouse, or a great tap dancer, you are primarily part of a couple. A couple which involves their loved one.

We know one woman whose husband had no family of his own, and so he "adopted" hers upon their marriage. Even though the marriage ended, "Steven" was still so loved by the family that he continued to participate in all family celebrations. More often, however, the family and friend welcome mat disappears when the relationship ends. Even if you were friends with your "ex's" sister or brother beforehand, that friendship often won't survive your breakup.

> Gina said:
> You really find out who your friends are when you break up with someone. When Sam and I broke up, his friends, who I had come to think of as mine too, refused to return my phone calls. It really hurt me, because I thought I'd be able to count on these friends for support during the hard times. I was totally shocked and unprepared to be rejected not only by Sam, but also by these friends.

> Chris said:
> Looking back, I realize that one of the reasons I was so attracted to Mary was because of her outgoing, fun loving family. I never had much of a family life growing up, and when I saw Mary's family I wanted to be a part of it. I didn't consider the likelihood that I'd no longer be welcomed when Mary and I broke up. I think I was more devastated by losing Mary's family than by ending things with her.

It is also unfair to force mutual friends to "take sides." You may feel that if you were friends first, they should be in **your** corner. Unfortunately, if you force them to choose between you and your former partner, you may find that you are the one who loses!

How Do I Know When I'm Ready To Start A New Candidate Search?

In business, if a search doesn't produce a good candidate, or if the top candidate turns the job down, the client and the recruiter might not gear up for another search right away. They will look at what might have hindered the search, and fine-tune the process before starting again. As a love recruiter, you need to reflect upon the search you just experienced before you rush out and recruit all over again.

If you didn't hire the candidate you wanted, you'll probably think all other candidates are less attractive, at least for awhile. After some time has passed, look at your past relationship and breakup using your business ability — that means no rage or finger-pointing!

▶ Paul said:
I initially blamed Inez for our breakup, but now I realize that she was only partly to blame. Much of it was my possessiveness and my jealousy. It took me a while to understand what I was doing wrong, but I'm in a new relationship now and it's working because I've learned to keep my control issues under control.

▶ Tim said:
I moved in with Phoebe because she was the first woman I'd dated in a long time who wasn't interested in a heavy commitment. She seemed ideal because she'd been married twice before and told me up front that she'd never marry again. But last year I started thinking about settling down.

> I realized that now I wanted marriage and a family, but Phoebe wouldn't even consider it. We began to argue about it all the time, and eventually I had to move out. It wasn't Phoebe's fault. She had been up front and honest about her wants and needs from the start. I'm the one who changed.

Sometimes, the search you conducted was masterful and your candidate selection was good, but the circumstances of the relationship caused trouble.

> ▶ Amy said:
> I thought Peter was my ideal candidate when I was in graduate school in New York, eight months before he moved to San Diego to take an executive job. But then we just grew apart — distance and changing lifestyles. We talked on the phone, but I only saw Peter in person at semester breaks. After a while, I realized that I didn't want to leave New York, and I didn't want to have the corporate lifestyle that Peter loved. We loved each other, but we'd grown in different directions and needed to find more suitable candidates. It was hard to do, but now that we are both involved with new people, I know we did the right thing.

Here are some tactics to consider before you start a new candidate search:

- ♥ Give yourself time to recharge your batteries.
- ♥ Seriously reassess your game plan for recruiting love.

- ♥ Think about your past relationship, but don't obsess over it. Don't play the "blame game," even if you feel it's justified.

- ♥ Be professional and sedate about your breakup. (This is tough, but it's important!) Don't even consider destroying your ex-candidate's property or reputation, or sabotaging his or her new relationship. The only reputation that you will destroy will be your own.

- ♥ Start making new memories! Don't frequent your "old haunts"—at least not right away.

- ♥ Don't drive your friends crazy with your distress! Of course you need (and deserve) support, but if you can't talk about anything besides your past relationship, try joining a dating success team (see Chapter 8). If you are totally grief-stricken, consider having some sessions with a therapist or counselor.

If you can't get past your dismay, you're not ready to start a new search. Your friends can help you, but there's a limit to what they can do.

> Marilyn said:
> Kathy was my best friend so I figured she wouldn't mind if I constantly told her about my breakup with Roger. But one day on our way home from shopping, Kathy blurted out: "I'm not going out with you any more if you say one more word about Roger. I care about you, but I've clocked whole days listening to you and I can't take it any more!" At first, I was shocked and hurt, but I realized that I'd become an awful bore. She wasn't a therapist — she was my friend, and I'd burdened her way beyond the call of duty.

How Can I Make My New Search Successful?

We can't say it enough: your dating log is your best tool for re-assessing yourself or your candidates when you're ready to start again. Read it thoroughly. Some of it will be sobering, but you'll probably find yourself laughing at some of it, too. Look at your Candidate Job Description and *You Company Profile*. What changes would you make now? Are you certain about what you want and need?

> ▶ Pat said:
> In looking over my dating log, I saw that I was initially attracted to Andy because he was a "wild and crazy guy," but now I know that I really need someone stable and reliable who will always be there for me. I adjusted my candidate job description and I am now steadily recruiting a new candidate. This time, I know that what I have is what I really want.

You may also find that your assessments were appropriate, but you still settled for something else.

> ▶ Carol said:
> I knew for sure I didn't want to be a mother, especially not a stepmother of someone else's children. But Stan was so cute and charming that I convinced myself that I could handle the every-other-weekend visitation of his two small children. The children's visits were pure hell — and we fought about them for days after they left. When I reviewed my dating log, I realized that I dreaded

> those weekends with the kids more than I enjoyed my time with Stan. The dating log helped me realize that this wasn't a good relationship. I tried hard to convince myself that I could deal with his kids, but on paper I could easily see that I just couldn't do it.

You might also find that you made the common mistake of thinking that someone might change or you could change them.

> ▶ John said:
> Betty assured me that she only drank "on occasions" — but she didn't tell me that every night was an occasion for her. She knew I didn't like it, but she insisted that her drinking rarely got "out of control" and I was making "too big a deal" of it. Even though my dating log clearly confirmed that Betty had a serious drinking problem, I ignored it. The last straw was on Thanksgiving Day at my mother's house. Betty got so drunk at dinner that she badly insulted my grandfather and picked a fight with my sister. It was painful to write about that evening in my dating log, but it made me realize that Betty wasn't going to change.

Your log may also show you that your feelings for your candidate were closer to friendship than true love.

> ▶ Jim said:
> Rosalie lived in the apartment across from me, and we spent lots of time together when neither

> one of us had dates. Even though we never formally dated, we went shopping together, looked after each other's pets, and were friendly with each other's families. One evening, during a particularly lonely time for both of us, Rosalie confessed that she had loved me for a long time. I liked Rosalie better than most girls I dated but I didn't feel "that way" about her. Still, I believed that we could make it work if we tried. It was awkward, and the physical side of things was a disaster. One day Rosalie said: "Jim, this just isn't working. Let's stop before we ruin our friendship." I was so relieved. The friendship Rosalie and I had was important to us, but it just wasn't romantic love. I'm thankful that Rosalie was smart enough to accept that. I am grateful every single day that we are still friends.

In business, it is a sign of strength and courage if you learn from your mistakes and go forward without repeating them. In your love search, it is also a sign of strength and courage to learn from your past relationships, avoid repeating bad patterns, and stop choosing the wrong person time after time. If you've selected your final candidate and your offer has been accepted — congratulations. If you're starting a new search, we know you'll reach your goal and have the success you want — it really is only a matter of time!

The Bottom Line

"Love does not consist in gazing at each other but in looking together in the same direction."
Antoine de Saint-Exupery

From the desk of: The Advice Sisters

TO: *You Company* Recruiter

FROM: Alison and Jessica

RE: Summary of Chapter 9:
        Selecting the Final Candidate

1. At some point, you will be ready to finalize this *You Company* search. You will:

    ♥ Make an "offer" to a candidate which is accepted and end this search.

    ♥ Choose a finalist from several, make an offer which is accepted and end this search.

    ♥ Make an offer to a candidate which isn't accepted and start a new search.

    ♥ End this search without finding any suitable candidates and start a new one.

2. Your instincts, and the notes in your dating log (compared with the *You Company Candidate Job Description* and your *You Company Profile*) will indicate how close a match you have.

3. If you've already made an offer but the candidate isn't working out well for the job consider the effects (emotional, practical, financial, and legal) before you end the relationship and/or your current search.

Summary Blueprint

From the desk of: The Advice Sisters

Today's Date: _____

At some point you'll be ready to make a choice:

1. You've found your perfect candidate and you make an offer.

I will complete this by: _____

2. You're ready to choose a candidate from among several finalists and make an offer.

I will complete this by: _____

3. After a candidate review, you decide that there are no finalists for this search. You end this search and gear up for a new one.

I will complete this by: _____

4. A candidate has accepted the job, but isn't working out. Consider all the ramifications before you either split up or put this candidate (and your relationship) on probation.

I will complete this by: _____

5. Go on to Chapter 10.

I will complete this by: _____

Action Memo

From the desk of: The Advice Sisters

TO: *You Company* Recruiter

FROM: Alison and Jessica

RE: Chapter 10: Your Recruitment Is Successful, Or, Next Steps To Take

Some Final Thoughts on Your Journey:

If you have read this book from cover-to-cover before you began looking for love, we wish you a search that is exciting, fulfilling, and swiftly successful. If you are still recruiting as you read this final chapter, keep at it and you will find your special love.

As we've said so many times (And guess what? We're going to say it again!) each search for love is unique. We can't say for certain when your search will be successfully concluded, but we are sure that if you work hard, you **will** reap the huge rewards! You have learned how to replace luck with the skills you use in the working world (planning, research, analysis, reassessment, and your own instincts).

The plan we we've laid out for you, if followed carefully, works exceptionally well. However, the nature of love is just like the nature of business — it is sometimes unpredictable, with unforeseen variables. Sometimes, even the most meticulous recruiters won't see success as swiftly as they had hoped.

Final Memo

From the desk of: The Advice Sisters

Recruiting love takes intelligence, optimism, introspection, faith in your abilities and in yourself, a willingness to try new ideas, and a realization that you're probably **still** going to kiss a few toads along the way. In both business and love, being perceived as a winner is a large part of success. If you **act** and **feel** confident and successful, others will think of you that way too.

We hope that you have learned from the true stories throughout the book. You too, can attain success if you follow the chapter-by-chapter steps maintain your dating log, and use your Action Memos and Summary Blueprints to keep organized and focused.

You are now at the end of *Recruiting Love*, but your search may just be starting. It will be unlike anything you have experienced before, because this time, you're going to recruit love with **new confidence, new skills** and a **new plan** for success! You are now in **control** of the dating process. Finding success in love is like success in all endeavors: uplifting, and ultimately worth the effort. All the research, all the phone calls, all the strategizing and targeting, all the interviewing, and even all that toad kissing will be worth it, when the *Recruiting Love* plan finally pays off for you!

Final Memo

About the Authors

Alison Blackman Dunham and Jessica Blackman Freedman are twin sisters and advice columnists. Their print and cyberspace columns are enjoyed by over 2.5 million people each week.

Look for them on the World Wide Web!

"Ask Alison" at Career Magazine:
http://www.careermag.com/newsarts/current/dunham.html

Advice for Intelligent Singles Bulletin Board:
http://www.InsideTheWeb.com/messageboard/mbs.cgi/mb37587

Cupid's Network at:
http://www.cupidnet.com/advice/

Wedding Solutions at:
http://www.wedding.co.za/

The "Wedding Belles" on BLISS E-ZINE at:
http://www.blissezine.com/home.htm

We'd love to hear from you! Please send us your questions, your comments or your success stories! Send your voluntary report to:
Cyclone Books
420 Pablo Lane
Nipomo, CA 93444
http://cyclone.8m.com
email: cyclone@lightspeed.net

Did You Borrow This Book?
Need a great gift for your other single friends?
Want to check out our other books for singles?

You can find *Recruiting Love* at your favorite local or online bookstore, or from Cyclone Books (888)678-3666.

Or send this page (or a photocopy) with a check or money order to: Cyclone Books; Att: Samantha Shapiro, VP, Sales; 420 Pablo Lane; Nipomo, CA 93444

Also available from Cyclone Books:

The Original Lovers' Questionnaire Book, by Lorilyn Bailey
Barbara DeAngelis called this book "a valuable tool to discover if your partner is the right one for you." Contains hundreds of questions — ranging from silly to serious — that lovers need to ask each other before making a big commitment. $12.95

The Little Book of Online Romance, by Lorilyn Bailey
Let the nation's foremost authority on Internet romance guide you through all the do's and don'ts of this exciting new frontier! Featured on over 150 radio shows. Don't enter another chat room without reading this book! $12.95

Love By Mail: The International Guide to Personal Advertising, by Richard Coté
Read the definitive book on personal advertising that *Christian Singles News* says, "will change your romantic life forever." Detailed examples of personal ad writing included, along with a directory of over 560 American and foreign singles publications. Highly recommended! $12.95

Shipping $1.50 per book.
Order before Christmas and get free shipping!